Determining the Form

Structures for Preaching

O. Wesley Allen Jr.

Fortress Press
Minneapolis

DETERMINING THE FORM
Structures for Preaching

Copyright © 2008 Fortress Press, an imprint of Augsburg Fortress. All rights reserved. Except for brief quotations in critical articles or reviews, no part of this book may be reproduced in any manner without prior written permission from the publisher. Visit http://www.augsburgfortress.org/copyrights/contact.asp or write to Permissions, Augsburg Fortress, Box 1209, Minneapolis, MN 55440.

Scripture passages are from the New Revised Standard Version of the Bible, copyright © 1989 by the Division of Christian Education of the National Council of the Churches of Christ in the USA. Used by permission. All rights reserved.

Cover image: © iStockphoto.com/Igor Skrynnikov
Cover and book design: John Goodman

Library of Congress Cataloging-in-Publication Data
Allen, O. Wesley, 1965–
   Determining the form : structures for preaching / O. Wesley Allen, Jr.
      p. cm. — (Elements of preaching)
   Includes bibliographical references (p.   ).
   ISBN 978-0-8006-0444-8 (alk. paper)
   1. Preaching—Textbooks. I. Title.
   BV4211.3.A4245 2008
   251—dc22
                              2008035738

The paper used in this publication meets the minimum requirements of American National Standard for Information Sciences—Permanence of Paper for Printed Library Materials, ANSI Z329.48-1984.

Manufactured in the U.S.A.

12   11   10   09   2   3   4   5   6   7   8   9   10

Determining
the Form

Elements of Preaching

O. Wesley Allen Jr., series editor

Thinking Theologically
The Preacher as Theologian
Ronald J. Allen

Knowing the Context
Frames, Tools, and Signs for Preaching
James R. Nieman

Interpreting the Bible
Exegetical Approaches for Preaching
Mary F. Foskett

Shaping the Claim
Moving from Text to Sermon
Marvin A. McMickle

Determining the Form
Structures for Preaching
O. Wesley Allen Jr.

Finding Language and Imagery
Words for Holy Speech
Jennifer L. Lord

Delivering the Sermon
Voice, Body, and Animation in Proclamation
Teresa L. Fry Brown

Serving the Word
Preaching in Worship
Melinda A. Quivik

Contents

List of Illustrations　　　　　　　　　　　　　　　　　　vii

Editor's Foreword　　　　　　　　　　　　　　　　　　　ix

Acknowledgments　　　　　　　　　　　　　　　　　　　xi

Chapter 1 • Why Form Matters　　　　　　　　　　　　　1
　　The History of Sermonic Form　　　　　　　　　　　3
　　Form and Function　　　　　　　　　　　　　　　　5

Chapter 2 • Unity, Movement, and Climax:
　　　　　Essential Qualities of All Sermonic Forms　　　7
　　Unity　　　　　　　　　　　　　　　　　　　　　7
　　Movement　　　　　　　　　　　　　　　　　　　9
　　Climax　　　　　　　　　　　　　　　　　　　　11
　　Conclusion　　　　　　　　　　　　　　　　　　　12

Chapter 3 • Case Study: 1 Kings 19:1-15a　　　　　　　15
　　Context　　　　　　　　　　　　　　　　　　　　17
　　The Narrative　　　　　　　　　　　　　　　　　17
　　Sermonic Claim　　　　　　　　　　　　　　　　18

Chapter 4 • Propositional Lesson Sermons　　　　　　　21
　　The Form　　　　　　　　　　　　　　　　　　　21
　　Evaluation of the Form　　　　　　　　　　　　　23
　　Case Study: 1 Kings 19:1-15a　　　　　　　　　　24

Chapter 5 • Exegesis—Interpretation—Application Sermons　　29
　　The Form　　　　　　　　　　　　　　　　　　　29
　　Evaluation of the Form　　　　　　　　　　　　　34
　　Case Study: 1 Kings 19:1-15a　　　　　　　　　　35

Chapter 6 • Verse-by-Verse Sermons　　　　　　　　　39
　　The Form　　　　　　　　　　　　　　　　　　　39
　　Evaluation of the Form　　　　　　　　　　　　　41
　　Case Study: 1 Kings 19:1-15a　　　　　　　　　　42

Chapter 7 • The Four Pages Sermon   47
   The Form   47
   Evaluation of the Form   51
   Case Study: 1 Kings 19:1-15a   51

Chapter 8 • Valley Sermons   55
   The Form   55
   Evaluation of the Form   57
   Case Study: 1 Kings 19:1-15a   61

Chapter 9 • New Hearing Sermons   65
   The Form   65
   Evaluation of the Form   68
   Case Study: 1 Kings 19:1-15a   69

Chapter 10 • Negative to Positive Sermons   73
   The Form   73
   Evaluation of the Form   75
   Case Study: 1 Kings 19:1-15a   75

Afterword: Beyond an Introduction to Sermonic Forms   79

For Further Reading   81

Notes   83

Illustrations

Figure 4.1 • The Propositional Lesson Form   20

Figure 4.2 • A Propositional Lesson Sermon on 1 Kings 19:1-15a   27

Figure 5.1 • The Exegesis—Interpretation—Application Form   30

Figure 5.2 • An Exegesis—Interpretation—
Application Sermon on 1 Kings 19:1-15a   37

Figure 6.1 • The Verse-by-Verse Form   38

Figure 6.2 • A Verse-by-Verse Sermon on 1 Kings 19:1-15a   45

Figure 7.1 • The Four Pages Form   46

Figure 7.2 • A Four Pages Sermon on 1 Kings 19:1-15a   53

Figure 8.1 • The Valley Form   54

Figure 8.2 • The Four Pages Form as a Variation of the Valley Form   58

Figure 8.3 • The "Lowry Loop"   59

Figure 8.4 • The Classic African American Form   60

Figure 8.5 • A Valley Sermon on 1 Kings 19:1-15a   63

Figure 9.1 • The New Hearing Form   64

Figure 9.2 • A New Hearing Sermon on 1 Kings 19:1-15a   71

Figure 10.1 • The Negative to Positive Form   72

Figure 10.2 • A Negative to Positive Sermon on 1 Kings 19:1-15a   78

Editor's Foreword

Preparing beginning preachers to stand before the body of Christ and proclaim the word of God faithfully, authentically, and effectively Sunday after Sunday is and always has been a daunting responsibility. As North American pastors face pews filled with citizens of a postmodern, post-Christendom culture, this teaching task becomes even more complex. The theological, exegetical, and homiletical skills that preachers need for the future are as much in flux today as they have ever been in Western Christianity. Thus providing seminary students with a solid but flexible homiletical foundation at the start of their careers is a necessity.

Traditionally, professors of preaching choose a primary introductory textbook that presents a theology of proclamation and a process of sermon development and delivery from a single point of view. To maintain such a singular point of view is the sign of good writing, but it does at times cause problems for learning in pluralistic settings. One approach to preaching does not fit all. Yet a course simply surveying all of the homiletical possibilities available will not provide a foundation on which to build either.

Furthermore, while there are numerous introductory preaching textbooks from which to choose, most are written from the perspective of Euro-American males. Classes supplement this view with smaller homiletical texts written by women and persons of color. But a pedagogical hierarchy is nevertheless set up: the white male voice provides the main course and women and persons of color provide the side dishes.

Elements of Preaching is a series designed to help professors and students of preaching—including established preachers who want to develop their skills in specific areas—construct a sound homiletical foundation in a conversational manner. This conversation is meant to occur at two levels. First, the series as a whole deals with basic components found in most introductory preaching classes: theology of proclamation, homiletical contexts, biblical interpretation, sermonic claim, language and imagery, rhetorical form, delivery, and worship. But each element is presented by a different scholar, all of whom represent diversity in terms of gender, theological traditions (Baptist, Disciple of Christ, Lutheran, Presbyterian, and United Methodist), and ethnicity (African American, Asian American, and Euro-American). Instead of bringing in different voices at the margin of the preaching class, Elements of Preaching creates a conversation around the central topics of an introductory course without foregoing essential instruction concerning sermon construction and embodiment. Indeed, this level of conversation is extended beyond the printed volumes through the Web site www.ElementsofPreaching.com.

Second, the individual volumes are written in an open-ended manner. The individual author's particular views are offered but in a way that invites, indeed demands, the readers to move beyond them in developing their own approaches to the preaching task. The volumes offer theoretical and practical insights, but at the last page it is clear that more must be said. Professors and students have a solid place to begin, but there is flexibility within the class (and after the class in ministry) to move beyond these volumes by building on the insights and advice they offer.

In this volume, O. Wesley Allen Jr. presents the challenge preachers face of choosing the rhetorical shape of the Sunday sermon week after week. Having determined what the text says, what the congregation needs to hear, and what she wants to say, the preacher must decide *how* to say it. A major element of this involves determining the *form* of the sermon, the ordering of ideas and imagery designed to convey a specific gospel message and offer a particular experience of that message to a particular congregation. The book begins with the foundational matters of why form must be consciously considered instead of intuitively developed and the basic elements of any form. The bulk of the volume, however, is a survey of various forms preachers have found effective over the years. Allen's survey is representative, not exhaustive. The collection is intended to provide a variety of approaches that beginning preachers can master and experienced preachers can use to expand their homiletical repertoire.

O. Wesley Allen Jr.

Acknowledgments

As editor of the Elements of Preaching series, it is tempting to use this opportunity to thank those who have supported the work of and contributed to the series in general instead of simply naming those who gave me aid in the writing of this specific volume. But in truth the distinction is flawed. The conversations I have had with other authors in the series—Ron Allen, James Nieman, Mary Foskett, Marvin McMickle, Jennifer Lord, Teresa Fry Brown, and Melinda Quivik—along with the reading I have done of those volumes that have preceded mine have influenced the approach and tone I have used in this volume in too many ways to name. They are some of the finest scholars and teachers I know and my work is better for trying to keep up with them. In addition, Ron Allen gave insightful feedback concerning my initial take on the task of teaching sermonic form, and David Lott, who edits all of the Elements volumes for Fortress, has been an invaluable conversation partner throughout the whole project. And I would be remiss if I failed to name the constant support I receive in this and all my work from my wife Bonnie and daughter Maggie.

Perhaps because of the introductory nature of this volume, I have, more than with any prior writing project, felt myself surrounded by a cloud of witnesses who have not only shared their faith and thoughts with me but have taught me to preach and taught me to teach preaching. Earl Gossett, Bill Muehl, Harry Adams, Fred Craddock, and Gail O'Day were my professors. Heather Murray Elkins, Jan Dunnavant, Lisa Davison, and Bill Kincaid have co-taught with me. And students from a range of backgrounds and with an array of vocational goals have sat with me in preaching classes at Drew Theological School and Lexington Theological Seminary while we explored ways to proclaim the most significant aspect or experience of God's forgiving and demanding presence in conversation with diverse congregations in diverse contexts. All three groups—professors, colleagues, and students—have taught me much about the task of proclamation. I dedicate this book to them, and pray that its publication may bring me into an even wider circle of sisters and brothers in Christ who can teach me yet more about the call not simply to preach the Word, but to effect a hearing of the Word.

O. Wesley Allen Jr.

Chapter 1

Why Form Matters

There are two major phases of sermon development or preparation. The first phase involves deciding *what* you want to say—choosing a biblical text; interpreting the text; determining the relation of the text to the needs of the congregation/world; settling on a sermonic claim that will engage the minds and hearts of the listeners at the most significant level. The second is deciding *how* to say what you want to say. This phase involves choosing language, commentary, metaphors, and imagery and placing them in some order that will best invite hearers to consider, engage, experience, assimilate, and live out the message of the gospel you are offering on that particular Sunday or worship occasion.

When the sermon is well developed, the what and how of the sermon are inseparable in the experience of the hearer. The language, imagery, and structure of the sermon do not call attention to themselves. Compare the experience to that of reading a novel. In reading a novel, readers need not diagram each sentence to make sense of them or outline the flow of ideas from paragraph to paragraph. In fact, readers pass quickly over a statement describing the villain's character, launching into a plot shift, or drawing a dialogue to an end *as long as* the structure and flow of the sentence or paragraph make sense. But for a sentence to pass by easily *and* meaningfully in the readers' experience, the novelist has to be intentional and oftentimes slow in writing the statement.

So whereas the what and how are inseparable for an audience, for the speaker or writer the two are distinct, ordered phases in the creative process. The how flows forth from the what. To confuse, merge, or reverse the two phases is to risk fulfilling the proverbial cliché of allowing the tail to wag the dog. We have all heard (and, to be honest, many of us have preached) sermons in which a how element supplanted the process of developing a clear significant what. In the experience of hearing the sermon there was a disconnect or just plain confusion. The process looks something like this. Reverend Harris hears a joke on Tuesday that has nothing to do with the text for the week, but it is cute so he uses it as the introduction of the sermon to get the congregation's attention. Or, during her first reading of the biblical text, the mention of fish sends Reverend Johnston's mind off to the story about her grandmother praying every morning beside her fish pond and suddenly the conclusion for the sermon is set although exegesis has barely begun. Or Brother Frank goes to a lament in the psalms looking for three points that will preach and so forces logical propositions of an argument out of a prayer expressing deep, emotional angst.

In sermon preparation, how must always follow what. If we are honest, however, the sermon preparation process is messier than such a linear description implies. Stories, quotes, ideas, and concepts for sermonic structures creatively pop up during the what phase. Preachers should not ignore or suppress these, but instead find a way to manage them. Jot them down on a separate notepad to the side to which you can return when you have finished your exegesis. Or type them into a separate document file so that you can evaluate them once you have clearly named your sermonic claim. The how encroaches upon the what in ways that can be beneficial as long as one learns to use the creative sparks in a way that they do not consume the what process.

On the other side of the coin, the preacher's sense of the what of the sermon is not set in stone once she turns to the how. Our understanding of and existential involvement with the content of the sermon continues to evolve and deepen as we consider how to offer the content to the congregation when we step into the pulpit. This is as it should be. Sermon preparation should be a dynamic, organic process instead of a to-do checklist. Time marches on from Monday to Sunday, but the sermon preparation process that moves with it does not march in a straight line or to a steady beat. We discipline the preparation process, but we never completely control it. It is more like a dance than a march. In the first phase, study leads creativity in the dance, but creativity is still influencing the dance steps. In the second stage, creativity leads, but critical study is still its partner. Hopefully, imagination inspired by the Holy Spirit is the melody to which the couple dances in *both* phases.

But if the what is changed too dramatically during the how phase, we should ask whether we are still developing the sermon we had intended. We may need to reenter the first phase and then restart the second. The tail can still take over control of the dog late in the process. Thus, generally (that is, linearly) speaking, the how phase follows (albeit in a messy fashion) the what phase in the preparation process so that the partnership of the what and how is inconspicuous and well balanced in the hearing of the sermon.

One of the most important considerations in deciding how to say what you want to say is to determine the form of your sermon. By sermonic form we mean

> the overarching rhetorical structure of the sermon—the intentional ordering of ideas and imagery designed to convey a specific gospel message and offer a particular experience of that message to a particular congregation.

The difference between sound theology, spiritual direction, or prophetic critique that simply hangs in the air of the sanctuary and an experience of the gospel descending into the minds and hearts of the congregation in the pews is often a matter of partnering the right message with the right form.

The History of Sermonic Form

The current state of the discussion of sermonic form actually had its origin in the late medieval period. The Franciscans and Dominicans began using a new form of preaching, usually referred to as the "university sermon." One fifteenth-century preaching manuscript uses the metaphor of a tree to describe this new form. From a very short trunk extend three major limbs. Then from each limb are three smaller branches. The approach is to take a central theme and break it into three points, each of which is then divided into three subsections.[1] This was the beginning of the three-point, two-joke, and one-poem sermon.

Another sermonic form that has had lasting influence on the North American pulpit and which is only a little younger than the university sermon comes from the Puritan Plain style of preaching. Arising in late-sixteenth-century Calvinism in England and New England, the form emphasized the exposition of Scripture. There are three major parts of the sermon: first, comment on the ancient text in its ancient setting; second, draw eternal, doctrinal points from the ancient text; and third, apply the doctrinal points to the current lives of those in the congregation.

While the Puritan Plain form is different than the structure of the three-point sermon, the logic is similar. Both forms are deductive, propositional approaches to proclamation. They move from general conclusions to specific applications and utilize didactic, persuasive language.

While there were certainly dissident, creative voices sounding in the pulpit here and there, these two basic homiletical forms (which we will discuss in later chapters) and variations of them have dominated most of preaching in the West for the last half millennium. In 1958, however, two voices arose that offered new insight into determining sermonic form in the sermon preparation process. One was that of R. E. C. Browne. In *Ministry of the Word*, Browne argues that the gospel should not be reduced to a standard structural formula (such as three propositions or interpretation followed by application). Instead, the sermon must authentically and artistically grow out of the character of the person preaching and relate to the form of revelation represented in the biblical text being preached. Preaching should be more artistic poetry than philosophical prose.[2]

Browne's voice was complemented by that of H. Grady Davis. In *Design for Preaching*, Davis expresses dismay that preachers take all aspects of the gospel and force them to conform to a single rhetorical form. Instead, he argues, "There is a right form for each sermon, namely, the form that is right for this particular sermon."[3] Sermonic form and content should be organically related. He uses the metaphor of a tree to express this insight, but his is a different sort of tree than the medieval preaching tree of the university sermon. According to Davis, a sermon should have one sturdy idea like the trunk, deep roots of research and reflection that are never seen, and branches that thrust out from the central trunk bearing fruit and blossoms appropriate to that tree alone.[4] So the sermon's content determines the appropriate form, instead of a standard form determining how all content must be presented.

In the 1970s and '80s, this sapling of form reformation transformed into an orchard. A group of homiletical scholars who have been grouped together under the label of the "New Homiletic" began making new proposals concerning form. Certainly, this movement involved much more than sermonic form. It dealt with the character and power of language, the role of the Bible in the pulpit, theology of preaching related to the New Hermeneutic—an approach to interpreting biblical texts associated with Rudolf Bultmann's students, Ernst Fuchs and Gerhard Ebeling—the character of African American preaching (especially the role of celebration), how people listen, and the role of media in shaping orality. But the discussion of rhetorical structure was a major component of it and was related to all of these other elements. Various approaches that were dialogical, inductive, and narrative in orientation sprang up.[5] Suddenly preachers were no longer working with one or two forms familiar to both preacher and congregation. The tried and true came to be considered trite and over-trodden. The homiletical conversation for the last thirty-five years has been dominated by this discussion of form as an organic and theologically central element of the sermon.

Form and Function

Preachers need multiple forms in their sermon preparation knapsack. Too often we get in a stylistic rut, using the same basic sermonic form week after week. The form, be it a three-point or narrative approach, is comfortable and expresses, we think, our preaching voice. But this understanding of style/form is a confusion of what is usually meant by the preacher's "voice" in homiletical discussions. The metaphor of voice in this context refers to the way each preacher brings her or his unique personhood and existential engagement of the Christian faith to bear on proclamation of the Word in any given sermon.[6] This voice changes only as the preacher changes, so there is continuity of voice from sermon to sermon regardless of theme, biblical text, or liturgical occasion. The form one uses, however, should change to meet the needs of the sermonic claim as it addresses a particular congregation in a particular liturgical occasion. Preachers bring their same "voice" into the pulpit regardless of whether they are preaching at a wedding directed to those gathered to hear vows more than a sermon, a praise service directed to seekers, or a traditional service directed to the longtime faithful. If preachers are inconsistent in voice, the gospel is represented as being incoherent. But to be consistent in form is not only to risk boredom but is insensitive to the particular needs of the congregation, the particular claim of the biblical text, and the particular demands of the liturgical context. A three-point sermon structure used on Sunday to make a didactic argument concerning some complex doctrinal or social justice issue should not be pulled out again on Wednesday when trying to comfort the family and friends of Charlie, who committed suicide at the age of thirty-two. By coupling a consistent voice with diverse sermonic forms from sermon to sermon, preachers invite hearers to engage the constant and trustworthy good news of Jesus Christ in its diverse manifestations.

It is important to remember that ultimately we are not called simply to preach the gospel but to get the gospel heard. In other words, while all Christians are committed to the content of the gospel, preachers are committed to it specifically *as* that content affects those gathered in the sacred assembly to hear it proclaimed. Different forms offer hearers different experiences of the gospel—different ways of thinking, of feeling, and of acting. All sermons should invite intellectual, psychological, and behavioral/ethical responses.[7] Different forms do this differently. This form primarily engages the hearer's mind, that one the hearer's heart, and another that person's hands. If we want our preaching to help our hearers love God with their whole heart, soul, strength, and mind, then we must utilize different forms that over time engage the whole person of the listener.

Chapter 2

Unity, Movement, and Climax
Essential Qualities of All Sermonic Forms

In the opening chapter, I argued that preachers need to be familiar with a number of sermonic forms so that during the sermon preparation process they can choose one that best serves the purposes of the sermon. I will spend the bulk of this book exploring various forms that preachers may use and adapt. But before turning our attention to these individual forms, we need to examine some broad considerations that concern all sermonic forms. These are rhetorical qualities that should be a part of every sermon regardless of the particular rhetorical strategy employed. These qualities are *unity*, *movement*, and *climax*.

Unity
We have all heard (and perhaps have at times been) preachers who preach a sermon that in truth contains two or three sermons within it or sermons that spend more time on side trips than on the primary homiletical journey planned for the day. Phrases like, "Back to what I was saying," "Let's return to . . . ," or, worse, "Where was I?" betray a lack of focus on the part of the preacher. Jumping from biblical text to biblical text, shifting from doctrine to doctrine, or wandering from issue to issue demonstrates a preacher's lack of preparation or, at least, clarity. From the congregation's side, such lack of focus in the sermon results in split attention. Some hearers may never return from a tangent to the main line of thought. Others may experience a disconnect when they are involved in the main claim of the sermon and then are asked to make a sharp turn toward an only loosely related idea. Or some may simply get lost in

the sermon, stay confused, and let their mind wander to any thing other than the good news of Jesus Christ.

Effective sermons require a strong focus. This has always been true but never more so than today. It is difficult to keep a congregation's attention in our contemporary, media-soaked world. We have become an attention-deficit society. We scan a Web site on our laptop with a mixture of animated images and text popping up at us while watching the evening news on the television that is filled with two-minute stories concerning politicians who talk in sound bites while headlines scroll across the bottom of the screen. We go to bed with the one-liners of late-night talk show hosts playing on the television and wake up to the one-liners of morning DJs on the clock radio. We listen to our iPods shuffling songs from album to album while reading a magazine that has every story broken apart by pop-out sections, photographs, and advertisements.

Preachers may be tempted to offer sermons that reflect this kind of flittering around from idea to idea. But, if it is to be transformative and life giving, the gospel requires a deeper level of involvement than we usually engage in with these other sorts of media. Thus, we must stay focused on some specific element of the gospel for a sustained time if hearers are to assimilate the good news and grow in the Christian faith. Because of the media-laden nature of our existence, however, the focus must be a narrow one. Hearers will mentally pop in and out of the message without us leading them out. Keeping a tight focus allows them to jump back in without being left behind.

In other words, a sermon today needs to say one thing, say it slowly, and say it well. From beginning to end, preachers need to stay focused on a single topic, theme, and/or scriptural passage. Sermons should be "simply significant"—simple but not simplistic. To keep from having multiple, competing messages in a sermon, we should write down our sermonic claim in a simple, declarative, theological sentence. Then we can test each paragraph or movement of the sermon to make sure it is supportive of this claim—either leading toward it, naming it, or unpacking it. If the sermonic claim focuses on Christology, make sure this paragraph doesn't slide into an ethical discussion. If the sermonic claim grows out of an exposition of a passage from the wilderness narrative in Exodus, make sure that paragraph doesn't stray into an interpretation of Paul's understanding of justification. If the sermon is aimed at offering a pastoral word of comfort, make sure the closing move does not turn into exhortation. Does every part of the sermon focus the hearers' attention where and in the manner you intend?

Movement

While sermons need to have a unity of focus, they must not be static. Hearers should experience sermons more like watching a movie than staring at a painting in a museum.[1] Movement is essential for keeping the hearers interested in what is being said and open to the transforming power of the gospel. Every sermon, regardless of its form, has a beginning, a middle, and an end. The relationship to the unified focus is different in each of these phases of the sermon. The beginning in some way hints at the claim that is to be offered. The middle unpacks and develops the claim in a way that draws hearers into a deeper understanding of the text, doctrine, or issue being discussed. And the end, in different ways, seals the claim in the hearts and minds of the hearers and hopefully influences their behavior.

To be honest, while all sermons start somewhere and end somewhere else, hearers often get left behind on the journey because the preacher has not planned the flow of ideas, exposition, and imagery as well as possible. We have all heard (and perhaps preached) sermons where thought B seemed to be completely unrelated to thought A that had just been spoken or where an example was offered that didn't seem to illustrate at all what had just been argued. There may well have been an important connection present, but it was evident only in the mind of the preacher. When we have been dealing with a biblical text and working on the sermon all week, things that seem clear to us will not be so to hearers who approach the text for the first time two minutes before the sermon begins. So preachers need to work carefully to construct a flow throughout the sermon that moves slowly and clearly enough that the hearers stay with the sermon the whole way.

Think of preaching as driving a car with the hearers in the back seat. As the driver you know where you are going and can take a sharp curve at a pretty fast speed because your body intuitively knows when and how to lean into the turn. But in the meantime those in the back seat who do not have a foot working the accelerator and brake or hands on the steering wheel are flung from side to side and get motion sickness. When we drive with someone in our car we have to pay more attention (than when we are alone) to easing into a stop at the intersection, slowing down on the curves, and not jerking our passengers when we hit the gas. So it is with preaching. The hearers need not know the final destination of the sermon from the moment it begins, but they do need to understand how each idea, statement, and image follows what just preceded and have a sense that it is preparing them for what follows immediately after.

Not only should the transitions in a sermon be relatively smooth (unless we *intend* to throw off our hearers for a short time for effect) but they should also be few in number. With passengers in the car, drivers may not only take curves a little more slowly than when they are alone, they may choose a route that has less curves to avoid the potential of motion sickness in the passenger. Likewise, we preachers want our congregations to experience some kind of shift in thought, attitude, and/or behavior during the sermon, but it must be one they can hold on to. This is best achieved by one primary curve or *hinge* in the sermon instead of many smaller (especially sharp) turns spread here and there throughout the sermon.

To shift away from the driving metaphor, Eugene L. Lowry asserts that one of the best ways to think about sermonic flow that will carry listeners along the whole length of the sermon is for preachers to develop sermons that move from an itch to a scratch.[2] In the opening of the sermon, the preacher raises some question or concern for the hearers—the itch. For some sermons, this will be a concern the congregation already has, and the preacher must simply name it. For others, the concern will be one the preacher wants the congregation to have and must create in them. On the Sunday after 9/11, no preacher in the United States had to create an itch. Every person sitting in the pew wanted to know what the gospel had to say in response to the violent attacks and tragic loss of life. What hope have we? Where is comfort found? What is to be made of God's promises? In the years that have followed 9/11, by contrast, many preachers have found their congregations to be less concerned about the wars in Afghanistan and Iraq than they would like. People follow the news, wondering what has happened and perhaps discussing at home or at work what should be done, but they have not brought this itch to church. The difference between the violence being in our backyard and halfway around the world allows us to hold to a false dichotomy between politics and religion. For many congregations, preachers who choose to speak prophetically the gospel's call for peace in the shadow of these wars in foreign lands will have to move slowly and carefully to create the itch.

This discussion shows how important the opening (or introduction) of the sermon is. Preachers often, mistakenly, assume they have to grab the congregation's attention by using some cute or funny story. Too often these types of beginnings have nothing to do with what follows. The opening must foreshadow what is to follow. The opening makes a promise that what is to come is worth listening to, worth committing some part of their being to. A joke about a minister, priest, and rabbi is rarely worthy of the moment (or of the gospel). This is not to say that no sermon should include or even begin with humor. Humor plays an extremely important role in service to serious matters. But beginning every sermon with a disposable joke to trick the laity into listening to something more important to follow does our hearers a disservice. Instead, the importance must be signaled or hinted at right from the opening in a way that piques the interest of the congregation. Whether we begin by referring to or retelling the biblical text, naming a recent event, telling a story, offering a question, or reciting a joke, we make the hearers a promise about what is to come. We name or create an itch and promise to scratch it.

Climax

The itch can begin to be scratched right after it is introduced, slowly bringing relief throughout the sermon from the tension raised in the opening of the sermon. Or the itch may need to be worsened throughout the sermon before a last-minute salve is applied to it. The flow from itch to scratch can take many forms, but if a scratch does not come, there is no good news regardless of how significant the itch is. Life questions deserve life-giving answers. Preachers do not have to have all the answers, but they should be able to offer an answer (a least a serious, tentative answer) to the very question they raise at the beginning of the sermon.

Whatever form the answer takes—whether the scratch comes slow and steady throughout the sermon or fast and furious at the end—how the sermon closes is essential to its effectiveness. The end of the scratch should be the strongest moment of the sermon. It must be stronger than the itch and serve as the exclamation point to whatever ideas, figurative language, and imagery has been used earlier in the sermon.

Earlier we spoke of the sermonic claim in terms of inviting the congregation to think, feel, and act upon some message. To be more specific, the sermonic claim is an expression of what preachers want the congregation to think, feel, and do at the *close* of the sermon. The end of the sermon, at which point the message fully "claims" the hearers intellectually, experientially, and ethically, is the climax of the sermonic event. This means the strongest imagery and/or the most provocative language should come at the close.

To put it as directly as possible, the beginning and middle of the sermon serve the ending. To return to our earlier metaphor of the journey, the climax is the destination, and should be the end, of the sermon. Preachers waste precious liturgical time, and the time of the individual listeners, when they take hearers on a Sunday drive to look around at a little spiritual scenery but then just return them to where they started. If they follow the model of the gospel, preachers should take hearers from one existential location to another—from guilt to grace, from apathy to action, from confusion to clarity.

But we should note that the climax of the sermon each week need not be earth shattering (although we celebrate when someone has such an experience of the gospel). We preach week after week and must trust in the cumulative effect of liturgy and proclamation on those who gather to praise God and seek to live a more Christ-like life. It is too much to aim for 180-degree turns in our hearers each week.[3] We should aim for smaller, more realistic transformations—changing an idea, more deeply understanding an issue, building stronger commitment to a principle, reforming a habit, opening where previously closed. A climax can be an internal "Hmm" as much as a spoken "Aha" or a shouted "Amen!"[4] The climax of every sermon need not be the high point of the hearers' week or even of the liturgy. But there must be a high point of the sermon, and it must come at the end.

One of the greatest (and most common) sins of preachers is not knowing when to end a sermon and thus ending in an anticlimactic manner. We have offered an image that exemplifies or encapsulates our claim, but then we just cannot resist adding one more comment, pulling it all together with a predictable question ("What is God calling you to do?"), or summarizing what we have said. It's like trying to explain, defend, or apologize for a joke after the punch line has been delivered. If a joke requires commentary, it either was not a good joke or was not told well. Similarly, at the end of a journey, the driver need not remind the passengers of where they have been or where they have arrived or reiterate why the journey was important or ask them whether they got the point of the trip. To do so diminishes the passengers' own experience of the journey. Indeed, it shows a lack of trust in the power of the journey and of the destination themselves. Preaching is the same. We should lead our hearers up to a climactic moment and then trust them and the gospel to do the rest.

Conclusion

Most of this volume is dedicated to exploring a variety of specific rhetorical structures with which preachers should be familiar. It may be helpful to use the forms somewhat strictly when first learning them in order to have a strong rhetorical foundation on which to build. But in reality sermonic form should not be viewed as static. These forms are not building codes that must be followed under penalty of law. Rhetoric is better understood as descriptive of what speakers have found to be effective than prescriptive of what *must* be followed if speaking is to be effective. Different sermonic claims call not only for different choices among basic forms but also different ways of *adapting* these basic forms.

When adjusting a form to serve our homiletical goals, we especially need to attend to the qualities discussed in this chapter. A sermonic form can only be effective so long as it brings unity, movement, and climax to the proclamation of the gospel. If the preacher does not attend to these three elements, the choice and adaptation of form will be moot. If we do attend to them, however, we will find our congregants engaged at a deeper level not only in our sermons but in the Christian faith journey itself. These elements are not add-ons to proclamation. They are its vehicle.

Chapter 3

1 Kings 19:1-15a
A Case Study

In chapters 4 through 10, we will examine a wide variety of sermonic forms. Each form will be presented as a diagram or flow chart so that readers get an introductory visual impression of the movement of the form and relationships of its parts. The logic and purpose of the form will then be explored. This will involve a step-by-step walk through the form to show how it works rhetorically and how a preacher works with it in the sermon preparation process. This general discussion of the form will be concluded with a brief evaluation of its strengths and weaknesses. To help make the form more accessible for preachers' consideration in sermon preparation, I will imagine how I might use the form if I were developing a sermon on 1 Kings 19:1-15a.

Given what I argued earlier about form growing out of the critical and creative process of studying a biblical text and developing a sermonic claim, forcing the same exegetical observations and a single sermonic claim into multiple sermonic forms is clearly an artificial exercise. I offer it less as a model of sermon preparation methodology and more as a heuristic device. By using a single case study to which I apply each form, we can see in more concrete ways the real similarities and differences between the forms described in this volume.

In order to prepare us for this element of each chapter, here I will offer a summary of exegetical observations on 1 Kings 19:1-15a and determine a sermonic claim for a congregation based on that interpretation. This passage is a familiar one to many and is the First Testament lection for Proper 7 of Ordinary Time, Year C, in the Revised Common Lectionary. It is primarily known for the scene on Mount Horeb where God comes to Elijah not in a great wind, earthquake, or fire but (in the traditional language of the King James Version) in a "still small voice" (v. 12). Many a sermon has been preached on God not coming to us with mighty, verifiable signs but in quiet ways we can easily miss if we fail to pay close attention. But a quick exegetical overview will show that more is at stake in this passage than the mode of God's self-disclosure.[1]

1 Kings 19:1-15

[1]*Ahab told Jezebel all that Elijah had done, and how he had killed all the prophets with the sword.* [2]*Then Jezebel sent a messenger to Elijah, saying, "So may the gods do to me, and more also, if I do not make your life like the life of one of them by this time tomorrow."* [3]*Then he was afraid; he got up and fled for his life, and came to Beer-sheba, which belongs to Judah; he left his servant there.*

[4]*But he himself went a day's journey into the wilderness, and came and sat down under a solitary broom tree. He asked that he might die: "It is enough; now, O Lord, take away my life, for I am no better than my ancestors."* [5]*Then he lay down under the broom tree and fell asleep. Suddenly an angel touched him and said to him, "Get up and eat."* [6]*He looked, and there at his head was a cake baked on hot stones, and a jar of water. He ate and drank, and lay down again.* [7]*The angel of the Lord came a second time, touched him, and said, "Get up and eat, otherwise the journey will be too much for you."* [8]*He got up, and ate and drank; then he went in the strength of that food forty days and forty nights to Horeb the mount of God.* [9]*At that place he came to a cave, and spent the night there.*

Then the word of the Lord came to him, saying, "What are you doing here, Elijah?" [10]*He answered, "I have been very zealous for the Lord, the God of hosts; for the Israelites have forsaken your covenant, thrown down your altars, and killed your prophets with the sword. I alone am left, and they are seeking my life, to take it away."*

[11]*He said, "Go out and stand on the mountain before the Lord, for the Lord is about to pass by." Now there was a great wind, so strong that it was splitting mountains and breaking rocks in pieces before the Lord, but the Lord was not in the wind; and after the wind an earthquake, but the Lord was not in the earthquake;* [12]*and after the earthquake a fire, but the Lord was not in the fire; and after the fire a sound of sheer silence.* [13]*When Elijah heard it, he wrapped his face in his mantle and went out and stood at the entrance of the cave. Then there came a voice to him that said, "What are you doing here, Elijah?"* [14]*He answered, "I have been very zealous for the Lord, the God of hosts; for the Israelites have forsaken your covenant, thrown down your altars, and killed*

your prophets with the sword. I alone am left, and they are seeking my life, to take it away." ¹⁵*Then the* Lord *said to him, "Go, return on your way to the wilderness of Damascus."*

Context

The author of Kings describes King Ahab as having done more "to provoke the anger of the Lord, the God of Israel, than had all the kings of Israel who were before him" (16:33). Given the low opinion the author has of most other kings, this is quite a strong statement. It is a response to Ahab's marriage to Jezebel and his efforts at combining worship of the God of Israel with Baal. God responded to Ahab's wicked ways by sending Elijah, who declared God's judgment in the form of a drought (17:1-7), which lasted for more than two years (18:1).

The drought ended only after Elijah challenged the 450 prophets of Baal to a contest on Mount Carmel. He and they would build altars to the ones they worshiped but not strike the fire. Whichever god lit the sacrificial fire miraculously would be recognized as the only true God. In spite of hours of invoking the name of Baal, crying out, and even bloodletting, the prophets of Baal received no response. Baal was shown to be impotent. Elijah then rebuilt an ancient altar, poured water all over the wood stacked on it, and prayed a simple prayer that God reveal Godself by lighting the fire. And God did. Elijah commanded the crowds watching to seize the false prophets and kill them (18:20-40).

The Narrative

Our passage opens with a reference to this contest and says that Queen Jezebel swore an oath that she would do to Elijah what he had done to her prophets (19:1-2). Suddenly the prophet who trusted in the omnipotent God to set water to fire and defeat 450 prophets of Baal turns scared and flees with his tail between his legs. He flees south, out of Israel into Judah with his servant, and then alone further south beyond Judah (vv. 3-4). Even hidden in the wilderness with a whole country between him and his accuser, the prophet of the Lord remains scared. He is ready to die, but God is not done with him. An angel (in Hebrew the word is simply "messenger")—who at first appearance in verse 5 could as easily be from Jezebel as much as from God; only in verse 7 does the narrator clarify that this is a messenger of the Lord—appears who feeds Elijah so he has strength for more journey.

After eating, he travels forty days to Mount Horeb (v. 8) The time reference and setting echo Moses' sojourn in the wilderness at Horeb/Sinai and thus the reader expects God to reveal Godself to Elijah as God had to Moses. Elijah hides in a cave (like Moses' cleft?), but God comes in and asks Elijah what he is doing there. Elijah explains that he is the only prophet left in God's service and that he has a price on his head. God does not acknowledge the content of Elijah's response and instead sends him out of the cave to the face of the mountain, for God will pass by (vv. 9-11). There is a wind, earthquake, and fire but God is not in those. But then there is "sheer silence" (NRSV; the Hebrew is almost, perhaps intentionally, untranslatable). Elijah recognizes this sign as God, for he humbly wraps his face when it occurs (vv. 12-13). God asks Elijah the same question as before—"What are you doing here?"—and Elijah gives the same answer, failing to recognize that a repeated question implies the original answer was unsatisfactory (vv. 13-14).

Indeed, God's response is an indictment of Elijah. God does not offer condolences or comfort. God refuses to allow him to seek sanctuary on the holy mountain. God's words are imperatives, "Go, return . . ." (v. 15a). Elijah is a hunted man and God sends him back to face his hunters. In fact, he sends him back to name Ahab's successor and even his own (v. 16).

It is this twist at the end, and not the sheer silence, that is the climax of the scene. This is a call narrative, or better, a *recall* narrative. The passage is about vocation more than revelation, although the two are certainly related in the scene. God reveals Godself not as an excuse for escapism from the world but as the command to face the troubling politics of the world with realism and faith.

Sermonic Claim

Having determined what the text says, the preacher must still decide what she or he will say. Most texts invite numerous sermonic claims. By the end of this particular sermon on this particular text, what simple, significant thing do I want this particular congregation to think, feel, and/or do?

For the purpose of our case study, I will use God's recall of Elijah to help focus the congregation's understanding of the church's mission. Drawing an analogy between Mount Horeb and the sacred assembly on Sunday morning, I want the congregation to think of worship ("going to church") not as a means of escaping the world but as a means of being equipped to serve God in the world, to deal with suffering, to confront oppressive systems characterized by political and religious corruption.

I do not see the (hypothetical) congregation as apathetic or lazy. Instead, I believe they are overwhelmed and fear they are unable to make any real difference in the big problems facing the world. I want to move them beyond this fear to feel empowered to do God's will, to experience trust in God's good will. And, when the sermon is over and done, I hope the congregation will, in God's name, act. I want them to seek out ways to fulfill God's call to take on the powers that be, which use discrimination, persecution, and violence to oppress those without power, and to reach out to those who suffer under such systems.

In each of the following chapters, we will examine how a particular form functions in the abstract and then see how it might work to achieve this particular sermonic claim based on this particular biblical text.

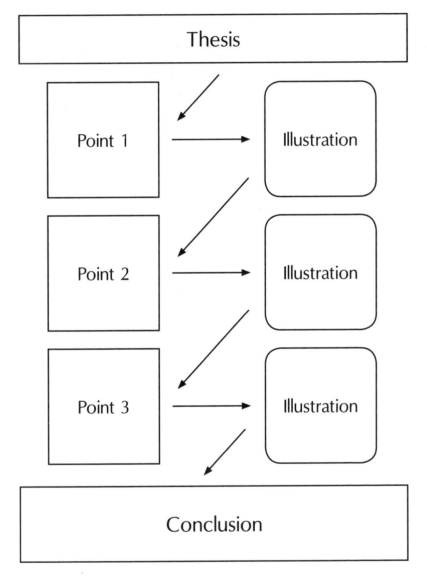

Figure 4.1 • The Propositional Lesson Form

Chapter 4

Propositional Lesson Sermons

In the opening chapter, we discussed the dominant role played by the sermon form that in the medieval period was called the "university sermon" and in more recent years has commonly been referred to as the "three-point sermon." This latter label is often used in a pejorative manner, so we are calling this sermonic form the "Propositional Lesson sermon" in hope that a new appreciation of the sermon type might be gained.

The Form

The Propositional Lesson sermonic form is deductive and topical in nature. By *deductive* I mean that the preacher states her primary theological assertion near the beginning of the sermon, and this general statement is then broken into smaller, particular propositions as the sermon unfolds. By *topical* I mean that the sermon is more thematically focused than exegetically oriented. This is not to say that Propositional Lesson sermons cannot be biblical sermons. Exegesis often plays an important role in the preparation stage, so that the preacher's primary thesis may be drawn from her theological-ethical reading of a biblical passage. But the structure of the sermon is based on a logic unconnected to the logic of the text. The preacher decides on a theme or topic that she develops into a primary thesis statement. From this topically derived thesis, she then extracts subpoints that are elements of the preacher's argument.

This last word of the previous statement, *argument*, I choose intentionally. This type of sermon is didactic, and as a teaching sermon the focus is on the intellectual aspect of the sermonic claim. The purpose of this form is to persuade hearers of the correctness of the point of view the preacher offers. It leads hearers deeper into the theological and ethical content of the faith.

As an argument, the sermon can work in one of two ways. First, the preacher can assume that all hearers will agree with the opening thesis statement. The focus of a sermon beginning with an agreed-upon claim is on the individual, more narrow propositions that follow. The preacher assumes these implications are not known or agreed upon by the congregation. He, therefore, tries to teach them about these implications and persuade them that they are true and important. The individual propositions may not be closely or directly related to each other but are all derived from the central claim. The logic is something like,

If A is true,
then B, C, and D are true.

For example, imagine you are preaching on 1 John 4:7-12. From the text, you take as your general, agreed-upon thesis the ethical statement that because God loves us we must love one another. You assume the congregation would agree with this general statement. But then you draw out the implications in terms of those to whom we do not usually extend Christian love. Point 1: We should love the non-Christian. Point 2: We should love enemies of our country. Point 3: We should love those who stand for positions we hate. These three points seem disconnected in flow, but they are all connected to the main thesis and have arisen in different ways in the church and in public discourse so they are connected in the congregation's experience.

Or, second, the sermon can work in the reverse. The preacher may propose a thesis that is not understood or accepted by the congregation. He then uses agreed-upon points to support this larger claim. Each point must build on the previous one if hearers are to be persuaded in a cumulative fashion. The logic of this type of propositional argument is that

A must be true,
if B + C + D is true.

For example, imagine you are preaching on Mark 13:21-33 during Advent. You know a number of your parishioners have been interested in Tim LaHaye and Jerry Jenkins's "Left Behind" book series. Some do not know what to make of the novels while others accept the authors' basic eschatological views. So you decide to argue for an experiential understanding of the New Testament's references to the *parousia*, or "second coming," as opposed to a literal, temporal interpretation. To persuade your hearers that this is so, you progress in the following way: Point 1: In the text, Jesus says both that we cannot know the time of the coming of the Son of man and that the parousia will occur before the generation to which he is speaking passes. This contradiction seems to raise intentionally a question about a literal temporal understanding. Point 2: The Greek word for time in verse 33 is *kairos* instead of *chronos*, "opportune time" instead of "temporal time." Point 3: We usually think of Jesus as *having come* two thousand years ago, but Christ is also always coming to us. Christ is both our past and our future.

The number of propositions used as subpoints in this form is variable. The best range is two to four points. You must have at least two or the thesis is not being divided into parts, but if you have too many points hearers will not be able to remember them. As the common label—three-point sermon—indicates, three points are most common. Patterns of three are common in speech and storytelling—for instance, the Three Little Pigs or the Three Bears—so congregations are culturally primed to expect three points.

Regardless of how many points are offered a congregation, they are usually offered in the same basic, deductive manner. The preacher transitions from the previous move of the sermon and introduces a new point, indicating in some way how it is connected with what preceded. Then she unpacks the point. She elaborates on its meaning using language that is meant to be persuasive, clear, and reasonable. She supports the point with evidence and logic drawn from a number of sources, including the biblical text(s) read in worship. Then the point is "brought home," if you will, through an image. It is in this type of deductive sermonic logic that imagery most fits the label "illustration." By use of a story, quote, metaphor, historical reference, or the like, the preacher gives some concrete flesh to the abstract proposition. Without the use of such illustrations, the sermon could almost be a theological or ethical lecture. But the illustrations help hearers assimilate the abstract theology or ethics and connect them to real life, that is, "apply" them to their very real lives.

Evaluation of the Form

Although the Propositional Lesson approach has dominated Christian preaching for nearly five hundred years, it has been the subject of much critique in the last half century, and for good reason. Or, to stay with the form, we can offer three good reasons. First, to reduce every biblical text—whether an epistle, apocalypse, prayer, prophecy, or narrative—to logical propositions, thesis, and subpoints, is to fail to recognize that the content of the passage is not so easily separated from its form. A psalm means in a different way than a pastoral letter means. Second, studies in the areas of communication and education recognize that today people do not learn and listen in a deductive mode as much as they do in an inductive manner. Sermons should better reflect the natural working of the minds of the hearers. And, third, too often multiple points really become multiple mini-sermons. Instead of a unified whole with three or so closely connected parts, in Propositional Lesson sermons hearers experience propositions as distinct, unconnected messages. This third critique is less directed to the form itself and more to how the form is often used.

The form has value, however. As Cleophus J. LaRue has argued, the three-point sermon has been and still continues to be more effective in the black church than white homileticians have often acknowledged.[1] Preachers often bemoan the ignorance in the pew of things biblical, theological, denomina-tional, liturgical, and ethical. In a post-Christendom, post-denominational day, the preacher must be concerned with teaching the faith. The Propositional Lesson sermon is essentially a teaching form. When the preacher intends to offer vital hearers information about some aspect of the faith tradition or persuade them of the importance of certain concepts and practices, this form may be of great help. If used too often, it is likely that hearers will mark time by the progression of points more than engage them. As the third point rolls around, congregants will begin thumbing through the hymnal for the next hymn. But if pulled out on the right occasion and used to address the right intellectual itch, this form may be the best vehicle for providing just the right scratch.

Case Study: 1 Kings 19:1-15a

Let us turn to the story of Elijah on Mount Horeb to see how we might use the propositional lesson form. Remember that my exegesis led me to read the text in terms of vocation and thus I chose to use the scene as a lens through which to interpret an element of the church's mission. Specifically, I am draw-ing an analogy between Elijah's fleeing to the Mount Horeb and the way some people come to church for escapist reasons, and I want to counter that under-standing of gathering to worship with an analogy drawn from God's recall of Elijah, or God's sending Elijah back down the mountain.

There are a range of ways this form could be developed to work with this sermonic focus. For example, I could offer the broad *thesis* in negative terms: we do not come to worship to escape the world. By expressing the general claim in the negative, I set up the hearers to experience the specific subpoints as positive. I will draw three positive lessons from the text and offer a coun-tervision to seeking escape in worship.

The *first point* grows out of a reading of God questioning Elijah in the cave and then again on the face of the mountain. God challenges Elijah: Why are you here? Elijah answers in terms of escapism, but God seems to reject the answer. So the first point is that we come to worship to be challenged or confronted by God. I will illustrate the point with a story of a woman in a church I once served who used to just say, "I enjoyed that message today, Pastor," every Sunday and then went home and I didn't see her again until next Sunday. But then one day she said, "Well, Pastor, today you went from preaching to meddling." She then showed up in my office Monday morning asking how to get more involved in the outreach of the church.

The *second point* grows out of God telling Elijah to go and return to the threatening place from which he just fled—we come to church from the world to be sent back out to the world. I would likely use this portion of the sermon to discuss that the "Sending Forth" part of the ordo is not just a tag-on, not just a way to get us out of the building quickly and off to Sunday brunch before the congregation across the street beats us to the restaurants. In some ways, the Sending Forth is the climax of the service. Everything leads up to the commission and benediction (and I would want to make sure the liturgy for that part of the service resounds with this claim when we get to it). To illustrate this point, I recall hearing a story of a preacher speaking to a group of college students. He inspires them with his preaching and then asks, "Are you ready to go out and serve God." They respond, "Yes." He asks again. They shout, "Yes!" He asks one more time, and the whole crowd is on their feet shouting, "Yes." And then the preacher says, "Good, I have buses waiting outside to take you to the local federal housing project."

The *third point* grows out of the specific instructions that God gives Elijah. These instructions come after the end of the reading as defined by the lectionary, but are clearly part of the scene. God tells Elijah to anoint Jehu to take the place of Ahab as king of Israel and to anoint Elisha as his own prophetic successor. The sermonic proposition is that as we are confronted in worship (connecting back to the first point), God sends us out to confront oppression and corruption in the world. To illustrate this point I would relate a story one of my students once told in a sermon. The church she was serving as a student associate minister had been discussing the possibility of starting a ministry to the rising immigrant population in their small town. One member who was a construction worker objected strongly, arguing that the immigrants were a threat to his job. A woman spoke up and said softly, "Bob, if you're scared, can you imagine how they must feel?" The church does now have a ministry to Hispanics, and Bob heads up the committee that advocates for just immigration reform.

In the propositional lesson form, the *conclusion* primarily serves as an opportunity to summarize the argument that has been made. So here at the end, I would return to the general negative claim and tie together the three positive responses to it. The summary would allow me to make a closing invitation for the hearers to embrace the vision of the church's vocation I have offered and to seek ways to embody it.

If we use the diagram of the form from the beginning of the chapter and insert our material, it looks like this:

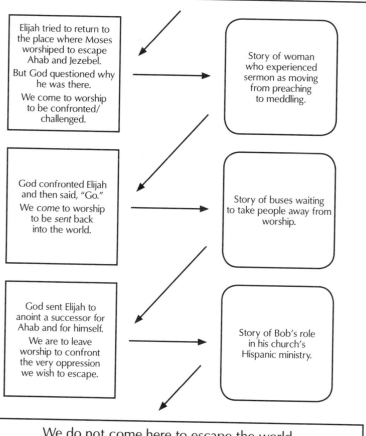

The church is not a means of escaping the world.

Elijah tried to return to the place where Moses worshiped to escape Ahab and Jezebel.
But God questioned why he was there.
We come to worship to be confronted/challenged.

Story of woman who experienced sermon as moving from preaching to meddling.

God confronted Elijah and then said, "Go."
We come to worship to be sent back into the world.

Story of buses waiting to take people away from worship.

God sent Elijah to anoint a successor for Ahab and for himself.
We are to leave worship to confront the very oppression we wish to escape.

Story of Bob's role in his church's Hispanic ministry.

We do not come here to escape the world,
but to be sent by God back into the world,
equipped to deal with oppressive forces.
How shall our church do this?

Figure 4.2 • A Propositional Lesson Sermon on 1 Kings 19:1-15a

Chapter 5

Exegesis—Interpretation— Application Sermons

As noted in the opening chapter, two sermonic forms have dominated the Christian pulpit for the last five hundred years or so. The first is the propositional sermon we discussed in the last chapter. The other was the Puritan Plain style of preaching. We turn to that form now (see figure 5.1, p. 30).

Instead of using the label that describes its origin, for the purpose of this chapter I have chosen one that names the way it functions: the first section focuses on *biblical exegesis*, the second on *theological interpretation*, and the third on *hortatory application*. This approach to preaching is primarily deductive, although the form works best when the opening exegetical section functions inductively. We will describe the form to reflect this mixture of inductive and deductive logic. Each of the three sections should take up approximately a third of the sermon, perhaps a little less if there is an introduction. But the emphasis is on the middle section. The exegetical portion sets up the theological interpretation and the hortatory application flows out of it.

The Form

Before jumping into the exegetical section, this sermonic form may start with an *introduction*. This introduction should not give away what is to come but should foreshadow it. The preacher may raise a concern that will be dealt with in the theological interpretation section based on the exegetical observations drawn in the opening. Suppose the sermon is on Job 19 and the preacher is going to address the issue of theodicy. More than give a defense of God's

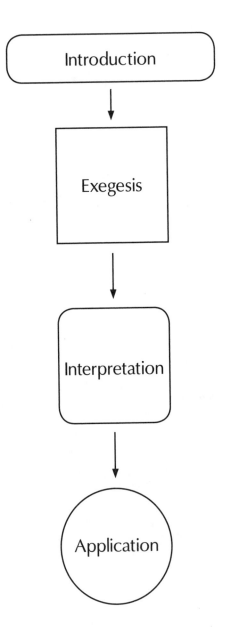

Figure 5.1 • The Exegesis—Interpretation—Application Form

righteousness, in this particular sermon she wants to affirm that questioning God can be an act of faith. In the introduction she can raise the question of theodicy directly—"If God is all-loving and all-powerful, why is there so much suffering in the world?"—or indirectly by using an image that evokes the concern in the congregation—"Martha was only thirty-two years old when her cancer was diagnosed . . ." Whichever type of introduction she uses, the preacher raises the question on the lawn but then spends some time on the front porch of the biblical text before crossing the threshold that leads into the house of theological interpretation.

Instead of a separate introduction, the preacher may simply want an introduction that is part of the exegetical section itself. In this case, the text has usually just been read in worship and the preacher begins by naming puzzlement about the text itself. "Job sounds awfully angry in this passage, doesn't he? He is angry. Angry at God for all that has happened to him. And angry at his so-called friends for telling him he shouldn't be angry at God. How does someone get so angry? How does someone get so angry that he questions, 'If God is all-loving, all-powerful, and all-loving, why am I suffering?'"

In the *exegesis* portion of the sermon, the preacher walks through the text, offering commentary on its meaning in its ancient context. There are, of course, several layers of ancient contexts for most biblical texts. The preacher should choose *one* of these contexts on which to focus. A preacher working on a sermon on a gospel text could focus on the historical Jesus, the early church's use of the pericope in its oral form, or the meaning of the passage in the final form of the narrative as shaped by the redactor/author.[1] To mix these is to split the congregation's focus and lead them down a path of confusion.

Another mistake preachers often make in this section (and in all sermons where exegesis is offered to the congregation) is to assume that offering biblical "commentary" means they must sound like a commentary (in other words, academic). There is a difference between what can happen effectively in a Bible study and in exegetically based proclamation. In a Bible study the text is the object of focus, but in biblical preaching the text is the lens that focuses our attention on God's good news for us. Moreover, reading a commentary with the eye is radically different than seeing the gospel expressed in a text with the ear. Preachers must describe the text in a way that is engaging in an oral context. This is rarely the occasion for discussing the Hebrew vocabulary in a passage and more the time to help hearers "see" what was at stake in or behind the text.

To set up this engaged, visualized hearing, the preacher will often need to offer some background. This background may be historical (for example, describing the threat of the Babylonian Empire to set up the commentary on one of Jeremiah's prophecies), literary (for example, reminding the congregation about Jesus' journey toward Jerusalem to set up the commentary on the story of the triumphant entry), or intertextual (for example, narrating the story of Abraham to set up the commentary on Paul's interpretation of Abraham's faith in Galatians). As background, this material should not be allowed to get out of hand. The focus of the section needs to stay on the central passage itself, and more than a paragraph or so of background will detract from unpacking the text.

For most passages, unpacking the text will mean walking through the text from beginning to end. Because most texts work inductively with the emphasis coming at the end, following the flow of the text will sustain the congregation's interest through the retelling and interpreting of the text. Of course, some texts work deductively with the emphasis at the beginning and an argument unfolding afterward, and others work in a chiastic fashion where themes or language are structured in a reverse parallel pattern ($A^1 B^1 C B^2 A^2$) so that the emphasis appears at both ends (in the manner of an *inclusio*) or in the middle. Preachers can unpack texts of these sorts so that the interest is sustained until the end of the section by taking a quick, wide-angle overview of the passage and then zooming in and then focusing on the element emphasized.

The section should work toward a conclusion, a point at which the preacher can state in a sentence or two what the central claim of the text is. This exegetical proposition will serve as a transition into the next section, that dealing with *theological interpretation*. One of the issues that will show up over and over throughout the following chapters is how the preacher moves from the ancient biblical text to our contemporary situation. This involves difficult hermeneutical decisions that are beyond the scope of this book. Our concern is the homiletical, usually analogical,[2] shift from referencing the text directly to showing its implications for people of the Book today. In this form, the shift takes place in two stages—theological interpretation and then application.

Thus, having walked through the particularities of the biblical reading and declared its "message," the preacher is ready to offer a broader theological or ethical interpretation of that message. This move represents a shift from an ancient to a contemporary expression of the faith, from describing a text's theology to offering the preacher's constructive understanding of some element of Christian doctrine. It is impossible, and indeed irresponsible to try, to reconcile the diverse voices in the Bible. When exegetically describing Paul's view of justification by faith alone (for example, Rom. 4:1ff.) in contrast to James's argument for the close relationship between faith and works (James 2:14ff.), the preacher must be true to the apostle's unique worldview. Or when presenting the prophet's call for beating ploughshares into swords in one place (Joel 3:10) over against the more palatable message of beating swords into ploughshares (Isa. 2:4; Mic. 4:3), exegesis must present the prophet's intent with as much clarity as possible. But when the preacher moves from the descriptive to the constructive task in preaching, she must seek to offer a unified Christian worldview. Biblical preaching is not simply repeating what the Bible says. Instead, it uses what is claimed in a particular biblical passage as a diving board into the waters of a systematic interpretation of the good news of Jesus Christ.

This means that while the exegetical section moved inductively toward a conclusion, the theological interpretation section (indeed, the remainder of the sermon) moves deductively, flowing out of that conclusion. To work inductively again would be to jolt the hearers back to a new starting point. Instead, the end of the first section is the start of the second. The proposition drawn from the text is translated into a theological claim that is then interpreted throughout the section.

How this interpretation unfolds depends on what doctrinal or ethical issue is being explored. But one element that will often be a part of this section is a discussion of the doctrine as it has been interpreted in the church's traditions. How does it appear in the creeds, in early church scholars, in the thought of the reformers, in the early writings of the denomination? Such a turn to church history helps address the theological illiteracy found in today's congregations, but that is not a sermonic end unto itself. The goal of drawing on traditional expressions of the faith is to help hearers understand the importance of a contemporary expression of the issue at hand. So any turn to tradition must be complemented by offering a recent interpretation of the issue. Whether this contemporary interpretation is evangelical, liberal, neoorthodox, process, or liberationist depends on the theological orientation of both the preacher and the congregation.[3] But to offer a systematic view of the faith week after week, it is important that the preacher be intentional about drawing on similar and appropriate conversation partners over time.

As preachers must be careful not to sound like a commentary in the exegesis section, we must beware turning this section into a theological lecture. Without "dumbing down" the issue, our task is, again, to help hearers "see" what is at stake, what is meaningful in the concept under investigation. The concept must be presented in a way that hearers gain existential insight into God, self, church, or world.

Such existential insight will serve as the basis for the third section of the sermon—*application*. While the second section is the focus of the sermon in terms of content, the third section is the climax in terms of the hearer's experience. Here the preacher "brings home" the message by showing that it has the potential to make a difference in the hearer's life. The hearers are invited to respond to the proclamation, to embrace it and live it. Here it is made clear that theology is no abstract, scholarly endeavor. Theology informs Christian existence.

Often this application section is hortatory in character. The congregation is exhorted to live in a way consistent with the theological or ethical issue that was explicated in the previous section. So there is often a shift here from intellectual- to behavioral-oriented proclamation. This means that this section is the point in the sermon where imagery related to contemporary life is most important. Images that make the good news come to life in the midst of real life "applies" the theology of the interpretation section to the world of the congregation. Only with verisimilar examples will hearers not only experience the sermonic claim in the context of the sermon but also in the context of life Monday through Saturday.

Evaluation of the Form

As with the Propositional Lesson form, the Exegesis—Interpretation—Application form's strength is in its ability to function didactically. This sermonic approach teaches the faith in ways many other forms do not. It allows preachers to connect Bible, church history, theology, and ethics in a way that both informs and inspires.

However, too often this type of sermon is more informational than inspirational. Without hard work that invites the congregation to see with their ears, this form can lead to boring, lecturesque occasions. Even worse, the sermon can become three separate lectures—an exegetical one, a theological one, and an ethical one—if the sections are not closely connected and the transitions between them are not smooth.

The most common problem with this form, however, is a corruption of it. Preachers today often reduce the threefold partition to two parts, omitting the theological interpretation section. The meat of the sandwich is removed and hearers are left with only two pieces of bread, and congregations definitely cannot live by bread alone. In this amputated form, the sermon opens with exegetical commentary and then moves directly to application. There are two problems with this curtailing of the form. First, without the intervening theological reflection, hearers are left to assume that the difference between our sociohistorical context and that of the Scriptures is negligible. While we may argue that God is unchanging and the human condition is by definition universal and thus is the same today as it was in biblical times, the circumstances in which the human condition manifests itself and in which God is found are radically different. Second, to move directly from exegesis to application disregards the wisdom of our forebears in the faith. It pretends, if you will, that we in the twenty-first century are the first to interpret Scripture and the faith to which it gave birth, with no need to give ear to those who passed down the faith from Abraham and Sarah, Miriam and Moses, the prophets, Jesus, and the apostles to us. But, in truth, our understanding of the faith, whatever theological camp we settle in, is conditioned by the traditions of biblical interpretation, theological analysis, and ethical reflection that have preceded us over the course of thousands of years.

Case Study: 1 Kings 19:1-15a

To consider the strengths and weaknesses of the Exegesis—Interpretation—Application form further, let us consider how we might preach a sermon based on the story of Elijah on Mount Horeb using this approach. Remember that my exegesis led me to read the text in terms of vocation and thus I chose to use the scene as a lens through which to interpret an element of the church's mission. Specifically, I am drawing an analogy between Elijah's fleeing to Mount Horeb and the way some people come to church to escape troubles in the world, and I want to counter that understanding of gathering to worship with an analogy drawn from God's recall of Elijah, or God's sending Elijah back down the mountain, to our being sent into the world for service.

Introduction: I could begin the sermon by raising questions about how Elijah looks in this text: "This doesn't sound like the Elijah I know. The Elijah I know was full of prophetic courage, spoke truth to power, and trusted God when even the laws of physics were stacked against him." I could then supply the appropriate background by reminding the congregation of the scene on Mount Carmel where Elijah defeated Ahab and Jezebel's herd of prophets of Baal. "But in today's reading, Elijah doesn't look brave or prophetic. He looks like a dog running away with his tail between his legs."

Exegesis: Naming this discrepancy in Elijah's character gets the congregation to the starting point of the text. This will allow me, in the exegetical section, to walk through the story from beginning to end, highlighting the narrative dynamics that would have been missed in a first reading of the passage. I would name the southward movement, the divine assistance in the wilderness, the arrival at the same mountain where Moses met God, and God's interrogation of Elijah. All of this would lead up to the point in the story where God sends Elijah back down the mountain. I would conclude the section with a clear statement like, "God would not allow Elijah to use holy ground to escape from the world. Instead, there on Mount Horeb, God replenished, refocused, and recalled Elijah for the difficult work of battling oppression and suffering in the world."

Interpretation: This section could begin by drawing the analogy between Elijah's attempted escape and the escapism found in some who come to worship. In the same breath, I would claim that God sends us out in the same manner that God sent Elijah. One of the reasons we come to worship is to be replenished, refocused, and recalled for doing God's work outside the church. Thus begins the deductive movement.

In my own tradition of United Methodism, I could remind the congregation of the early days of the Wesleyan movement. In class meetings, participants were not simply comforted, they were questioned: "How is it with your soul?" The questioning was meant to hold those in the movement accountable to one another so that they would be empowered to live out the faith in difficult times. Moreover, John Wesley was not only concerned with the character of people's souls, but also with the state of their material and physical existence in England. Many of his writings, sermons, and works were aimed at addressing the ills of the Industrial Revolution. Methodists are by heritage people who work to alleviate oppression and suffering.

Application: How this section is developed depends a great deal on the specific congregation to which I am preaching. If my assessment is that the church is living up to this calling, I will want to praise and encourage them in their work. I will draw imagery from the life of the congregation to inspire more of the same. On the other hand, if my assessment is that this area is a shortcoming of the church, I will want to exhort them to claim this mission as their own. In this case, I will need to draw imagery from similar churches that can serve as models, especially churches that are not outwardly focused and have found a way to make outreach an important part of their identity.

If we use the flow chart of the form from the beginning of the chapter and insert our material, our sermon looks like this:

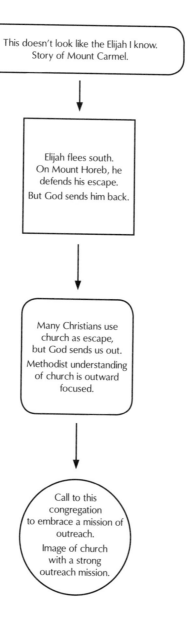

Figure 5.2 • An Exegesis—Interpretation—Application Sermon
on 1 Kings 19:1-15a

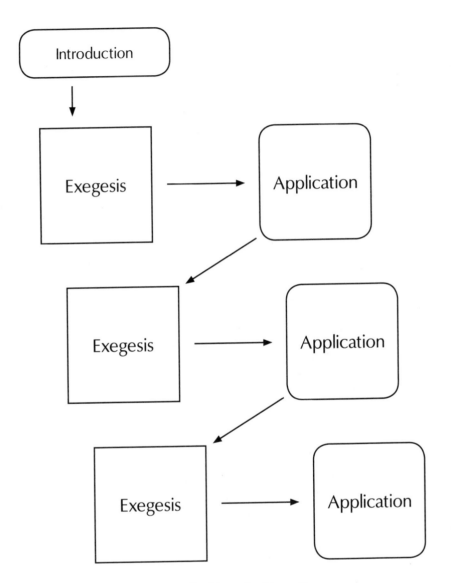

Figure 6.1 • The Verse-by-Verse Form

Chapter 6

Verse-by-Verse Sermons

In the early church, one approach to preaching was *lectio continua*, that is, working through a biblical text verse by verse, sermon after sermon. One legacy of that homiletical approach is the Verse-by-Verse sermonic form. Sometimes called expository preaching (although this term is also used in other ways), this sermonic form, as it has evolved, basically works through the biblical text for the day from beginning to end, allowing the structure of the text to determine the structure of the sermon.[1]

The Form

This sermonic form works in a pendulum fashion, moving back and forth between exegesis of the text and its application. I am using "application" here in the broadest sense of describing the contemporary relevance of the ancient text, not the more narrow sense used in the Exegesis—Interpretation—Application form. In this form the application sections of the sermon really collapse theological interpretation and connection to the contemporary situation into one element. The assumption behind this is that there is an easy (not necessarily simplistic) move to be made between the text and the contemporary situation of the hearers, that an analogy between the manifestation of the human condition and of God's addressing that condition in the text on the one hand and contemporary expressions of the human condition and the gospel on the other is readily available.

So this form works as a sort of running commentary on the passage for the day. This does not mean that the sermon engages in the kind of technical exegesis we find in a biblical commentary. This is a homiletical commentary, with a narrow, specific audience/congregation in mind. Although this approach is called expository, the goal is not simply exegetical description of the text. The goal is proclamation of the gospel. Commentaries explain, they do not proclaim. Running commentary, therefore, is the form, not the purpose.

To use this sermonic form, preachers must identify the major divisions of the text. Verse-by-Verse is really a misnomer. Versification of the Bible has only been around since the Middle Ages. These chapter and verse divisions were made for the sake of common reference and do not necessarily reflect the structural logic used by the original author. Thus, the occasional sermon of this type may divide the passage in accordance with individual verses, but more often each move of the sermon will focus on longer sections of the passage made up of several verses.

By following the structure and flow of the text, this sermonic form allows the text to determine the logic of the sermon itself. Most biblical texts unfold in an inductive manner, especially narrative passages. The "punch line" is at the end—God gives the rainbow as a sign of the covenant, Solomon receives wisdom, Jesus heals the Canaanite woman's daughter, or Jesus answers a question with a parable. Verse-by-Verse sermons on such passages work inductively, allowing the text to reveal its emphasis at it own pace. There are, of course, biblical texts that function deductively—a prophetic passage that opens with a general critique of religious practice in the face of social injustice and then unpacks it, or an epistle passage in which Paul makes a broad theological or ethical claim and then supports it. Using this form to preach on texts such as these will result in deductive sermons. In Verse-by-Verse sermons, the form of the passage provides the skeletal structure of the sermon.

Having named that fact clearly, it is important to recognize that there is more often than not no single, correct way to divide a biblical text. Different readers may understand the logic to unfold in different ways. This is because texts are by their very nature multivalent. There are a number of different ways to read a passage legitimately (while there are also numerous ways to read a passage illegitimately). How we read (as exegete) and how we decide to present the passage (as preacher) will lead to different divisions.

Our overall reading and preaching strategy will also influence how we should begin the sermon. Rarely should we jump right into the text. The preacher has been dealing with the text all week but the congregation has just heard it read for the first time. They come to it cold. An *introduction* is needed. We must provide an entry point for them, must create in them a desire to enter the text. Even though we do not want to give away the ending of the sermon, we want to begin creating an itch that will justify the detailed attention we are about to give the text.

Once the preacher has done this, she moves to the *opening of the passage*, perhaps summarizing it or retelling it in her own words. This must be more than a report of content. It must be creative and engaging, it must something that can be seen with the ear. The passage must be presented in a way that (1) highlights the need for explanation and (2) raises some level of suspense or expectation about what follows in the text (and the sermon). The first element is to be fulfilled immediately during this section of the sermon—characterization described, vocabulary explained, so on and so forth. The second element, of course, is fulfilled only slowly throughout the sermon.

Once the opening of the text has been presented and interpreted, the preacher moves to the *parallel application*. The function of this move should be the same as the parallel in the passage. If the opening of the passage raises a question in its historical, literary context, the opening application should raise the same question in our contemporary context. If the opening introduces a theological issue, the opening application should introduce it into the current context. Imagery, metaphors, and stories are used to make the analogy between the text and the hearers real, to give it flesh and bone and breath.

The preacher must make sure not to give away too much in the opening application. There are other moves to come. The role here is to set those up. As there is continuity between each section of the biblical text, the preacher must ensure that there is continuity across the different applications. Better, the preacher should not create multiple applications but one application that develops in phases, just as the text unfolds in phases. This does not necessitate that there be a single image used in parts throughout the application sections (although this is certainly possible) but that a single, sermonic claim be developed across the sections of the sermon.[2] Indeed, the initial application should lead to the next section of exegesis.

This pendulum structure progresses through the *divisions of the biblical text* toward the climactic, *final application* section of the sermon. The movement is not simply back and forth between exegesis and application but also forward from opening to ending. In the final application, the sermonic claim is most fully expressed by the preacher and experienced by the congregation.

Evaluation of the Form

The Verse-by-Verse sermonic form's greatest strengths is that it draws on the form and logic of the biblical text itself instead of forcing the biblical message into a form that is foreign to it. The preacher allows the passage to speak to today's church on its own terms, in its own way. The preacher plays the role of mediator, but the text is meant to be in control. As such the form does much to counter biblical illiteracy. The congregation walks through the details of the passage in a way that helps them learn, understand, and assimilate it.

Another benefit of learning this form well is that it can be used as part of a sermon instead of determining the whole structure. Every biblical sermon that at some point turns to the passage for the day must find a way to present that text for the hearers. A running commentary that is reduced in length and detail to serve the function of that moment in the sermon can be extremely helpful to hearers trying to grasp the significance of the text in the unfolding logic of the sermon.

On the other hand, this form is not appropriate for all occasions. In this form, the text is the controlling factor. If the starting point for the preaching occasion is a pressing social or pastoral issue, this is probably not the form to use since its primary focus is on the text. Instead of going to the text with a specific question in mind, this form moves in the other direction—it determines what are the important questions and the best answers.

A different problem with this form has been noted earlier. Preachers can easily allow the *divisions* of the text to win out over the *unity* of the text. As a consequence, the applications become disconnected and result in multiple mini-sermons. This weakness is not inherent in the form and is avoidable, but it is one that often occurs.

Case Study: 1 Kings 19:1-15a

To consider the strengths and weaknesses of the Verse-by-Verse form in a real example, let us return to the story of Elijah on Mount Horeb. My exegesis led me to read the text in terms of vocation and thus I chose to use the scene as a lens through which to interpret an element of the church's mission. Specifically, I want to draw an analogy between Elijah's flight to Mount Horeb and the way escapism motivates some people to come to church, and I want to counter that understanding of gathering to worship with an analogy drawn between God sending Elijah back down the mountain and worship empowering us to return to the world to serve the suffering and to counter oppression.

The *major divisions* of our pericope are easy to determine based on change of setting. The first section is verse 1, which provides the reason this scene occurs at all—the victory over the false prophets on Mount Carmel. The second comprises verses 2-9a, Elijah's fleeing from Queen Jezebel. The third is the conversation and divine revelation on Mount Horeb, verses 9b-14. And the final section is verse 15, where God sends Elijah back down the mountain to face that from which he fled. I would use these four sections of the text to structure the sermon.

To get into the text, I could use an *introduction* that helps the congregation identify with Elijah and the true-to-life manner in which he represents both great faith and great fear: "Do you ever wake up in the morning with such faith in God that you think you can take on the world? And you do. Until about noon, when everything that was going for you turns against you. Instead of taking on the world, you want to escape from it. Has that ever happened to you? You might not be proud of it, but you're not alone. Elijah could have started a Twelve-Step support group for people like us."

This beginning creates a slight itch in the congregation in a playful manner and sets up the first section of the biblical text. I would remind the congregation of what the *first verse* says and use it to rehearse briefly the story of Elijah defeating the Baal prophets on Mount Carmel. In the *parallel application* then, I could shift from the use of the second person in the introduction to third-person examples of people exhibiting the faith in difficult situations—someone speaking up when someone tells a racist joke, another joining a protest for immigration reform that is both just and merciful, and/or another helping a child get away from abusive parents.

These images of courageous faith lead back into the *second section* of the text where Elijah loses his courage. Even though he defeated 450 prophets of Baal, when he hears that Jezebel has put out a contract on his head for killing her prophets, he turns, puts his tail between his legs, and runs . . . out of the country . . . through Judah . . . through the wilderness. He would rather die out there than at the hands of the powers that be. He only survives because God wills it. In the *parallel application* I could use parallel imagery to that in the first to show that we flow back and forth between courage and fear in our faith. Specifically, we come to church and pray about those things instead of confronting them in the world—we pray that all God's children be treated equally but say nothing when we hear a sexist joke; we pray about the sanctity of life but only watch protests against capital punishment on the news; or we pray for those who suffer but when we suspect spouse abuse next door but are not sure, we look away and say that what happens in someone's home is private. Following the flow of the text, the itch is intensified.

This escalation leads into the *next section*, which is Elijah's conversation with God on Horeb. I want to keep the focus on Elijah, not on God's quiet revelation. So I tell the story in a way that emphasizes Elijah's tone. He defends his running away. In the *parallel application* I would talk about a common defense in our day. One that is heard often in this globalized, postmodern world is that problems are just too large for individuals or churches to have an impact on them. Too many people are poor and hungry. There is too much violence. There are too many people and institutions that benefit from the status quo: men, whites, the rich, rulers, multinational corporations. We can't do anything but pray.

Identifying this sense of helplessness leads into the *final section* of the text. God doesn't praise Elijah for what he had done in the past, nor does God comfort the prophet in his fear. God sends Elijah back down the mountain, back to face the troubles he was trying to escape. Drawing on what follows the lection, I would name that God instructs him to anoint Jehu to take Ahab and Jezebel's place on the throne and to anoint Elisha as his own successor. This would lead to the *climactic parallel application*, in which I could name that we come to worship not to escape the problems of the world or even simply to pray about them. We come to be sent back out into the world, empowered by God's Word, to confront people, powers, and systems that oppress God's children. I would close with an image of an individual Christian, a small group of faithful, or a church who prayed and was emboldened, then acted and made a difference.

If we use the diagram of the Verse-by-Verse form from the beginning of the chapter and insert our material, our sermon looks like this:

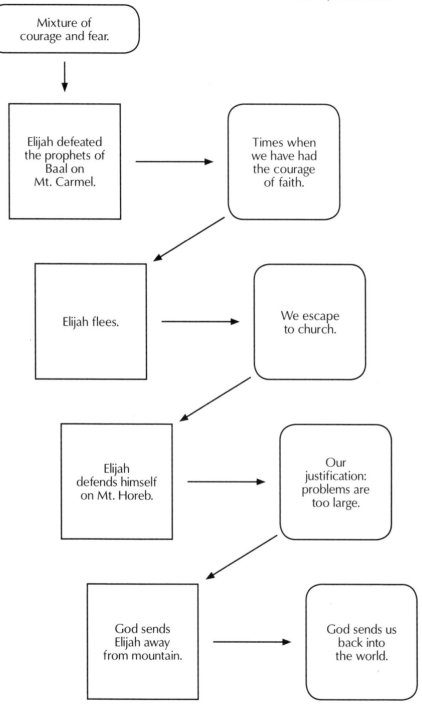

Figure 6.2 • A Verse-by-Verse Sermon on 1 Kings 19:1-15a

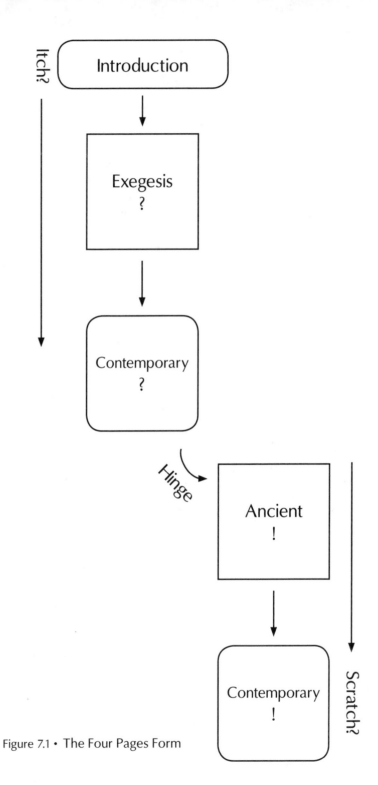

Figure 7.1 • The Four Pages Form

Chapter 7

The Four Pages Sermon

In 1999, Paul Scott Wilson published *The Four Pages of the Sermon: A Guide to Biblical Preaching*.[1] While the book discusses a range of issues such as hermeneutics, imagery, and a weekly sermon preparation schedule, our interest is primarily in the Four Pages structure Wilson proposes. This sermonic form represents a bridge between the last two forms examined (Exegesis—Interpretation—Application and Verse-by-Verse) and those that follow. Like the forms we have already examined, it moves from the ancient text to the contemporary context by way of direct analogy. Like the forms to follow, it flows inductively. An itch is developed without the hearers knowing how it will be scratched. Moreover, like the sermonic forms from this point on, this approach has a clear turning point in which the direction changes, a hinge that shifts from focusing on the problem or question (i.e., the itch) to the resolution or answer (the scratch).

The Form

The Four Pages sermonic form is a structure that reflects the strength of the law-gospel approach to preaching rooted in Reformation theology. It moves from human problem (sin) to divine answer (good news) but does so in a way that the hearers stay engaged because they do not know the destination at the beginning of the sermon.

The term *page* here is metaphorical. It refers to the structure of the sermon, not the length. Four pages indicate that there are four primary movements of this sermonic form. But as we have already mentioned, the sermon really travels in two directions, so the first two pages are paired for the leg of the journey through the problem and the second two for the leg through the good news.

An *introduction* may be needed to set the journey in motion, to help the congregation frame the itch that is about to come. Like any introduction, it should be so closely related to the first page of the sermon that hearers will not experience it as a separate move.

The *first page* focuses on the problem described in or lying behind the ancient biblical text for the day. Because it is the first major move of the sermon, this is the point where literary and/or sociohistorical background is offered to help readers get into the world of the text. The preacher may introduce the text quickly in a wide-angle fashion and then zoom in on the primary focus of the page—the expression of sin the text addresses.

This element of the human condition may be explicit or implicit in the text. Because we preach on short pericopae, the reading may not always include the whole story. Preachers may have to look to the broader context, or even to their wider theological understanding of the gospel to identify what aspect of the human sinfulness is being addressed in the lesson for the day. For instance, if the reading is one in which Paul addresses justification, the preacher may have to back out of the passage to see how Paul describes the sin that needs to be justified. Usually, however, there will be enough description of the problem—be it explicitly named, presented in a character's action or disposition, or hinted at metaphorically—in the pericope to deal with. In narrative texts, for instance, this element will usually be present in the first portion of the passage. Consider scenes from the Gospels. In a healing story, the illness and situation described in the opening of the text describes the brokenness of humanity. Or in a pronouncement story, the question posed to Jesus, the conflict that arises around Jesus, or the situation Jesus observes presents something of the human condition that will be addressed in the material that follows. On Page One the preacher exegetically and theologically unpacks this element.

On the *second page* the preacher moves via analogy to the manifestation of that aspect of sin, of the human condition, in today's world. The preacher not only extends or "applies" the theological understanding of the element to the context of the hearer, but provides imagery that allows hearers to experience it. The preacher "films" the problem in the world so that hearers do not observe it at a distance but recognize their own involvement with, participation in, or affliction by it. At this point, on Page Two the hearers find that the text names their lives.

With the move to the *third page*, there is a distinct change in direction. This change must be presented so that hearers experience it as being in continuity with, as proceeding from, the first leg of the journey while at the same time recognizing that the focus has shifted. The preacher returns to the ancient text to elucidate how God addresses the human condition named on the first page (and continued on the second). The first half of the sermon has been the set-up for the second half. We began with the bad news *so that* we can now proclaim and hear the good news with all its force.

Again, the particular manifestation of grace God offers in relation to that described on the first page may be explicit or implicit in the text. A pericope for the day could focus only on Paul's description of sin, but Paul's theology does not stop there and neither can the preacher. Our task is to proclaim the gospel, so we must look ahead to Paul's fuller argument (or in other situations to our fuller understanding of the ways that God is *pro nobis*—"for us") to share a message of the divine address. But, again, usually there will be enough description of God's salvific, providential care for humanity— be it explicitly named, presented in a character's action or disposition, or pointed to metaphorically—in the pericope to deal with. In narrative texts, for instance, this element will usually be present in the last portion of the passage. Consider scenes from the Gospels—Jesus heals, blesses, forgives, and instructs at the close of the pericope. Jesus almost always gets the punch line (either in speech or action), and this type of element is the focus of Page Three.

The *fourth page*, like the second in relation to the first, moves by way of analogy from the ancient description of grace to a vision and experience of the gospel in today's world. Again, for this to occur effectively, imagery must be employed that "films" the reality of grace. To "tell" about grace but fail to "show" it is to leave God buried in the pages of the ancient text while the human condition is seen around every corner.[2] The imagery used here need not be part two of the imagery used on the second page (although it can be). It must, however, be related. The same dynamics of the human condition imaged on Page Two must be addressed by God's good grace on this page. Page Four will not need a follow-up conclusion. Because it brings the divine answer into the contemporary world, it serves as the conclusion itself. Any summary or concluding thoughts added at this point would be anticlimactic.

The order of the Four Pages sermon as I have described it thus far is similar to the pendulum approach found in Verse-by-Verse sermons—moving from text to parallel, contemporary "application" and then doing it again. However, the order of the pages in this form is flexible and can be changed based on the sermonic claim that the preacher develops and how she views rhetorical structure as best serving that claim. Pages Two and Three could be reversed so that the order is:

Page 1—Ancient Problem
Page 3—Ancient Answer
Page 2—Contemporary Problem
Page 4—Contemporary Answer

This rearrangement basically results in a variation of the Exegesis—Interpretation—Application form. Here the preacher works through the text focusing on the human condition and the divine answer and then shifts to contemporary manifestations of the same human condition and the same divine answer. This way the primary hinge is not between problem and solution but between ancient and contemporary.

Another option is to reverse Pages One and Two. The resulting flow would be as follows:

Page 2—Contemporary Problem
Page 1—Ancient Problem
Page 3—Ancient Answer
Page 4—Contemporary Answer

In this rearrangement the focus is on the contemporary context with the text itself serving as the hinge between the human problem as expressed in today's world and God's answer as offered in today's world. This is similar to the Valley sermonic form we will examine in the next chapter.

While the flow of the pages is flexible, Page Four should be always the final and climactic movement of the sermon. Moreover, regardless of how the pages are ordered, for the form to be most effective, we must make sure that the connections between the different pages are strong. These connections are not difficult to manage but they are somewhat complex. On the one hand, there is a connection based on chronology. There must be continuity within the pages dealing with the ancient text (Pages One and Three) and within those dealing with the contemporary context (Pages Two and Four). On the other hand, there must be continuity within the pages dealing with the human condition (Pages One and Two) and within those focused on the divine response (Pages Three and Four).

Evaluation of the Form

The primary strength of the Four Pages sermonic form is its simplicity. This is a reliable form that can be pulled out of the preacher's toolbox any week to serve the hearer well. If the preacher has done her exegesis but just cannot get over that midweek hump toward the pulpit, this form can save the day (Sunday, that is). She must ask of the text, What is the (explicit or implied) human problem and what is the (explicit or implied) divine answer? Determining these two elements gives her the "thesis statements," if you will, for the first and third page. Then she must draw an analogy between the text and contemporary life, determining first how this particular aspect of the human problem manifests itself today and second how God's answer to that problem is revealed today. These decisions will provide the thesis statements for Pages Two and Four. The preacher then has her basic structure in place.

This simplicity can also be viewed as a weakness of the form. Viewing every biblical text in terms of sin → grace or law → gospel is somewhat reductionist. The kinds of meanings proffered by and the intended function of biblical passages range greatly. For example, while psalms of praise and epistolary paranesis are certainly related to our being saved from sin, they are really about other aspects of the human, religious experience. To force such texts into a problem → solution mode is to diminish the full scope of the Christian faith.

Case Study: 1 Kings 19:1-15a

To test out the Four Pages sermonic form on a concrete example, let us return to the story of Elijah on Mount Horeb. Remember that my exegesis led me to read the text in terms of vocation and thus I chose to use the scene as a lens through which to interpret an element of the church's mission. Specifically, I am drawing an analogy between Elijah's fleeing to Mount Horeb and the way some people come to church for escapist reasons, and I want to counter that understanding of gathering to worship with an analogy drawn from God's recall of Elijah, or God's sending Elijah back down the mountain. The Four Pages form can work well with this dual analogy.

As an *introduction*, I could begin the same way I proposed for Exegesis—Interpretation—Application, that is, raising questions about how Elijah looks in this text: "This doesn't sound like the Elijah I know. The Elijah I know was full of prophetic courage, spoke truth to power, and trusted God when even the laws of physics were stacked against him." I could then supply the appropriate background by reminding the congregation of the scene on Mount Carmel where Elijah defeats Ahab and Jezebel's herd of prophets of Baal. "But does Elijah look different in today's reading, or what?" A small itch is created that is intensified over the next two pages.

On *Page One*, then, I could show Elijah's journey from Carmel to Horeb, focusing on the difference in his speech on the two mountains: "What a difference a mountain makes! On Carmel Elijah is the epitome of courageous faith. But on Horeb he is scared and defensive. Nearly scared to death. He comes to the place where Moses met God, hoping to escape from the royal wrath."

On *Page Two*, I could draw a direct correlation to the contemporary situation. An expansion of the following or a story reflecting the following dynamic would work: "I guess we shouldn't be *too* hard on Elijah. We've all experienced the pendulum of faith and fear. We've all woken up in the morning with such faith in God that we think we can take on the world only to have our faith fall apart by noon. We believe we should speak up when someone tells a racist joke, we want to join a protest for immigration reform that is both just and merciful, we are convinced we could help a child get away from abusive parents. But when our fears arise, we decide to pray instead of act. We come to church to escape from the real world, to find comfort in the face of all the suffering, the violence, the hatred, the corruption in the world. The God of mercy will surely offer us solace."

Page Three will signal a shift of direction: "But you know, God didn't take Elijah deep in the cave where no one could find him and say, 'There, there, Elijah. I'm here for you. When there was only one set of footprints, that was me carrying you. I'll carry you now. You just lay your head down and quit worrying.' God said no such thing." Then I could focus in on God's instructions to Elijah, when God sends him back down the mountain to face his fears with faithful obedience. I would point out the irony that this is good news.

On *Page Four*, I would create a climactic experience of God's gift of this calling to us today. To do this, I could offer a story of someone who overcame fear to make a difference in the world. For the story to work, the church would need to play a role as God's instrument in empowering the person instead of being a community that simply offered the person refuge. Such transformative stories abound in the church.

If we use the drawing of the Four Pages form from the beginning of the chapter and insert our material, our sermon looks like this:

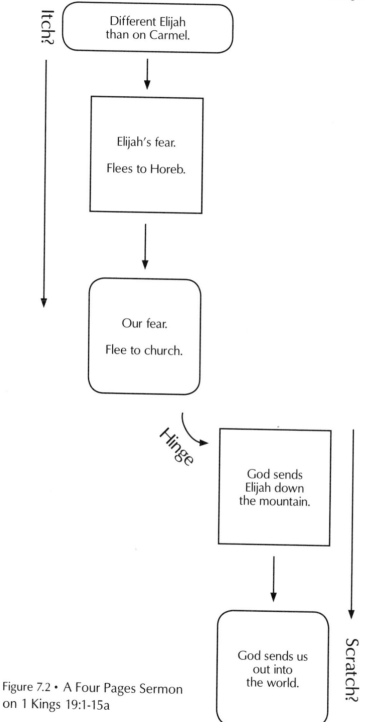

Figure 7.2 • A Four Pages Sermon
on 1 Kings 19:1-15a

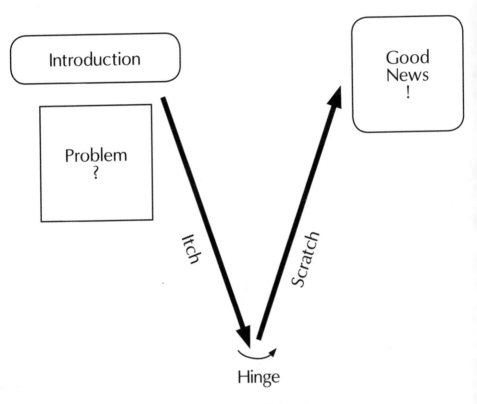

Figure 8.1 • The Valley Form

Chapter 8

Valley Sermons

The Valley sermonic form is simple in structure but is emotionally complex. The preacher takes a congregation down into the depths of an issue, problem, or question and then brings them up with the good news that addresses, solves, or answers what was introduced in the first half of the sermon.

The Form

The Valley sermonic form moves inductively from itch to scratch. What makes the form especially effective is the way the preacher lingers over both the itch and the scratch.

The sermon begins with an *introduction* of the itch. The itch can be of a range of types, such as an ethical issue (abortion), a theological question (theodicy), a sociopolitical situation (poverty), or a personal struggle (guilt). How one introduces the itch depends on whether the preacher assumes the question is one the congregation already holds or is one she wishes to raise for the congregation. If the issue is one on the minds of the hearers, the preacher simply needs to name it in a way that allows them to acknowledge it. On the other hand, if the question is one to which the listeners have not given thought (for instance, a social justice issue the preacher thinks is important but to which the congregation is inattentive), the preacher will have to introduce the topic more slowly, getting them to care about the topic and seeing it as important for themselves, the church, or the world.

Regardless of which of the above scenarios exists, once the issue is introduced, the first movement of the Valley works in the same way. The preacher slowly takes the congregation down deeper into the painful, distressing, or confusing concern. The *descent* is less intellectual in terms of thoroughly explaining the complexity of the question, although this may play a role. Instead, it is an experiential descent. The preacher uses imagery to deepen the hearers' existential concern with the subject matter. The imagery often takes the form of a litany of small images strung together. The preacher's concern is less that any of the images alone have an impact on the hearers and instead is working toward a cumulative effect. Example is piled on example with each one going deeper into the subject matter and deepening the hearers' psychological, existential desire for resolution. For example, imagine you are preaching on Romans 6:15-23 and your goal is to proclaim sanctification as God's continual salvific works in our lives. You could begin by demonstrating the need for God's continuing salvation. You might introduce the itch with a distant, easy-to-swallow description of the ancient church's debate about apostasy after baptism. Hearers might consider the debate silly—of course, we're still sinful after baptism. But then you start showing ways we who claim to have been justified through Christ's death and resurrection continue in sin. The movement could descend from little, innocent lies to our willful participation in systems that oppress others so that we reap benefit.

Once the preacher has taken the congregation down deep enough, to the point where they are leaning forward in the pews longing for an answer to the question or problem that they have now claimed as their own, the preacher must move toward offering a scratch. Too quick of an answer will not be effective given the slow descent. So a *hinge* must be offered that will introduce the reversal of the first half of the sermon.

This is the point where the preacher usually brings in the biblical text for the day. From the text the preacher draws the ethical-theological perspective she wants to offer the congregation. Assuming the text was read earlier in the service, the preacher will need to remind the listeners what the text is about (walking through the story, summarizing the argument) and in the process or afterwards offer an exegetical insight that leads to a statement concluding the section, one that names the sermonic claim in its most explicit form.

But naming the claim at this moment is simply an intellectual element of the sermon. Having experientially descended into the valley of the problem, exegetical and/or theological discourse will not get the hearers back up the other side. For the *ascent* truly to scratch the itch created, the preacher must offer imagery that allows the congregation to experience the good news as more powerful than the imagery through which they experienced the problem. This is the most important part of the sermon. The imagery in this half of the sermon may involve a string of images parallel to those used in the descent. More likely, however, an extended, developed narrative image is needed to overcome the negative experience in the first half of the sermon. It may open with the dynamic experienced in the descent but move quickly toward the resolution, answer, or solution to that dynamic. One wants to end the sermon with a climactic image that involves a situation or character with whom the hearers can identify and thus experience God's grace, providence, or call in a transformative manner.

Let us return to our example of the sermon on sanctification as Paul describes it in Romans 6:15-23. If the descent slowly moved from the ancient debate concerning postbaptismal sin through our peccadilloes to our deepest offenses, how might you invite hearers to experience something of God's continuing redemption in our lives? In the hinge you could quickly offer a wide-angle glance at the primary orientation of Paul's argument in Romans 6:1—7:6 and then zoom in on the passage for the day, focusing on what Paul means by sanctification. On the basis of this biblical rationale, you climb back out of the abyss of our sin with the hearers on your back by naming for them, showing them a significant, real-life example of God's sanctification in and of Christian existence—something like a church elder with a drinking problem who experiences sanctification in the form of reconciliation after a serious fallout in the congregation or a woman of faith who is consumed by materialism until God works through the church to place her as a volunteer in a homeless shelter and her perspective is sanctified.

Evaluation of the Form

The Valley sermonic form is a simple structure that offers great potential for engaging hearers intellectually and emotionally and inspiring a behavioral response. Its strength can be seen in the fact that what I have described above is really the skeleton of several other common homiletical approaches.

In the last chapter we examined the Four Pages form, with its dual parallel between the problem in the text (Page 1) and the problem today (Page 2) on the one hand and the good news in the text (Page 3) and the good news today (Page 4) on the other. As I mentioned, the order of the pages is somewhat flexible. When the first two pages are reversed, we basically have a variation of the Valley (see figure 8.2, p. 58):

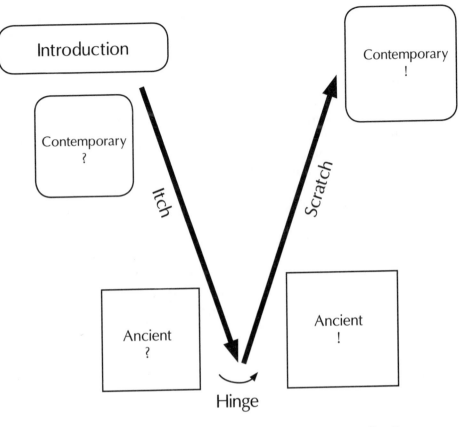

Figure 8.2 • The Four Pages Form as a Variation of the Valley Form

The Valley is also a simplification of the "Lowry Loop," the structure Eugene L. Lowry proposes in *The Homiletical Plot: The Sermon as Narrative Art Form.* Lowry offers an approach that moves through five stages (fig. 8.3).

The first move is to create the itch for the hearers—get them engaged by developing some ambiguity that will need to be resolved. Lowry calls this upsetting the equilibrium. The second stage involves digging deeper into ambiguity to determine all that is really at stake. Here the preacher and congregation analyze the discrepancy between what is and what can or ought to be. All narratives to some degree move toward an ending that resolves the conflict created earlier in the story. The third stage of Lowry's narrative sermon discloses the clue to that resolution without giving it away all at once. It's an "Oh, I get it" experience of reversal. This revelatory moment in the sermon leads the hearers to an experience in which the radical discontinuity between the world's way of thinking and the gospel is seen and felt. Here listeners hear

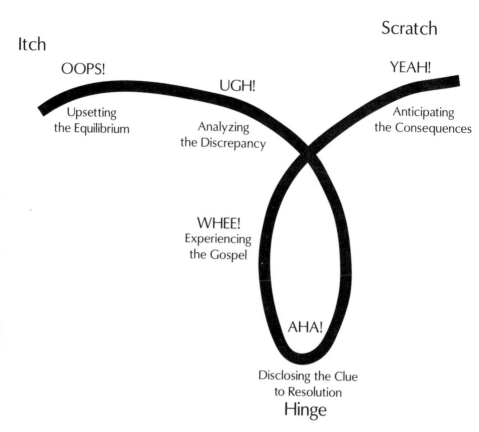

Itch

OOPS!

Upsetting
the Equilibrium

UGH!

Analyzing
the Discrepancy

Scratch

YEAH!

Anticipating
the Consequences

WHEE!
Experiencing
the Gospel

AHA!

Disclosing the Clue
to Resolution
Hinge

Figure 8.3 • The "Lowry Loop"

the good news proclaimed explicitly and find that the gospel is continuous with human experience as long as human experience has been turned upside down. The final stage is the anticipation of the consequences of embracing the gospel in the future after the speaking of the sermon is done. The hearers must decide for themselves what difference the gospel will make in their lives. Lowry's shorthand terms for the five stages are Oops!, Ugh!, Aha!, Whee!, and Yeah![1]

Finally, the Valley form shares much with the classic style of the African American pulpit. In *Come Sunday: The Liturgy of Zion*, William B. McClain lists ten characteristics of black preaching. One is that "Black preaching is characterized as slow and deliberate to a build up."[2] This characteristic describes the style in terms of speed, tone, and movement. McClain cites the traditional formula used by many black preachers: "Start low, go slow, go high, strike fire, sit down." The approach named in this formula is not simply about a technique of sermon delivery but also has implications for form. The form is characterized first by a slow, deliberate movement that allows the mind and heart of the hearers to become fully engaged. Then a dramatic shift in tone and pace occurs as the preacher moves toward the climactic ending of the sermon, which involves hope and optimism. All of the forms discussed in this book can and have been used in this approach, but the inductive Valley form is an especially close relative. Consider how the classic formula looks in diagram form:

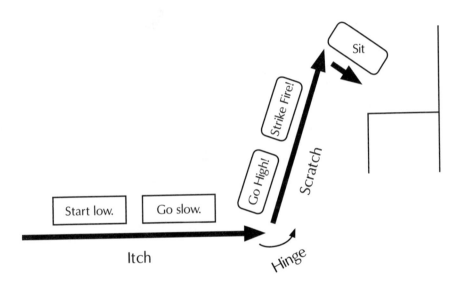

Figure 8.4 • The Classic African American Form

The primary weakness of the Valley sermonic form is the difficulty with creating an ascent that is able to overcome the experience of the descent. Too often we show hearers the problem with force and then simply report the good news.[3] I remember a Valley sermon on Philippians 4:4 ("Rejoice in the Lord always; again I will say, Rejoice.") by a young preacher. He introduced the itch by questioning the naïveté of Paul in calling his readers to *always* rejoice and compared the Greek word for rejoice (*chairō*) to Karo Syrup. Paul's exhortation seems rooted in a syrupy, sweet theology that ignores the painful reality of life. And then the preacher descended into that reality by naming recent stories in the news that showed the violence and brokenness of human existence. Each news story took us further and further away from rejoicing. Then for the hinge the preacher explored the context of Paul's letter to the Philippians. He played on the fact that Paul wrote the letter while in prison facing possible death. Paul's was no pie-in-the-sky, simplistic worldview. Paul is proclaiming the goodness of God over against anything the world can throw at us. And then the preacher applied that message to us in hortatory fashion. He *showed* us the ills of the world but only *told* us to rejoice in God's sovereignty. The first half of the sermon was greatly effective, but at the end of the sermon we were, experientially speaking, still in the depths of the human condition and were left to pull ourselves out.

Case Study: 1 Kings 19:1-15a

How might the Valley sermonic form be used to preach on the story of Elijah on Mount Horeb? My exegesis led me to read the text in terms of vocation, and thus I chose to use the scene as a lens through which to interpret an element of the church's mission. Specifically, I am drawing an analogy between Elijah's fleeing to Mount Horeb and the way some people come to church for escapist reasons, and I want to counter that understanding of gathering to worship with an analogy drawn from God's recall of Elijah, or God's sending Elijah back down the mountain.

For the Valley form to work for this sermonic claim, the descent and ascent cannot focus on the actions of escaping and sending themselves but those things from which we want to escape and to which God sends us out. With the *introduction*, however, I could begin at that point with something like, "What a week this has been! It sure is nice to be here away from it all. The music, the prayers, the fellowship, the font all just wash away the concerns of the world . . . even if for just an hour. It's no wonder we worship in a sanctuary. We come here seeking sanctuary from everything out there."

The *descent* begins as I describe the things "out there." I could organize a litany of images in terms of increasing seriousness. Or I could couple this movement with a move from smaller to wider circles of life from which we feel the need to escape—home (relationship problems with spouse, children, or parents), school/work (pressure to perform up to expectations), local, national (elections driven by corporations), international arenas (genocide in Darfur). A refrain—something like, "I'm sure glad we're in here and not out there"—could tie the litany together.

I could then walk through and interpret Elijah's story in terms of the shift from his fleeing from Jezebel to God's sending him back to anoint a successor to Ahab as the *hinge*. The refrain could be echoed in the fleeing part—"I'll bet he was glad to be in that cave and not back out there"—and then transformed after God sends him back—"God asked Elijah, 'What are you doing in here when I need you out there?'"

This could become the basis of the new refrain for the *ascent*—"We come here because God needs us out there." I could work through short, parallel examples of showing Christian impact on the home, school/work, local, national, and international arenas. Each example would be followed by the refrain. But whereas the litany in the descent half of the sermon led to the hinge, the litany here would need to lead to a climactic image that begins with some person or group seeking sanctuary in church only to find themselves challenged and empowered to face and transform a situation that needs the church's care. For instance, I could share the story of a woman who was a mother and youth minister at a Catholic church. Her eldest son, Casey, was raised in the church. Everyone who watched him as an altar boy thought he would become a priest. He was in college when the United States went to war with Iraq, so he signed up to be a chaplain's assistant. But Casey was assigned elsewhere and died in Iraq. His mother was devastated, buried her son from the church, found comfort in Mass. But she also found strength—the strength to camp outside of President Bush's ranch in Crawford, Texas, and start an antiwar movement. Shaping a story like that of Cindy Sheehan's faith, loss, and activism could help hearer's experience the possibility of responding to God's call to move from the pew to the world week in and week out.

If we sketch out this sermon in terms of the diagram of the Valley form, it would look like this:

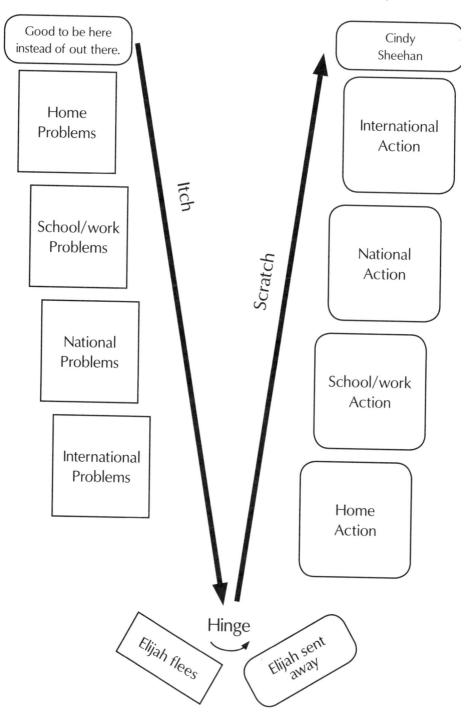

Figure 8.5 • A Valley Sermon on 1 Kings 19:1-15a

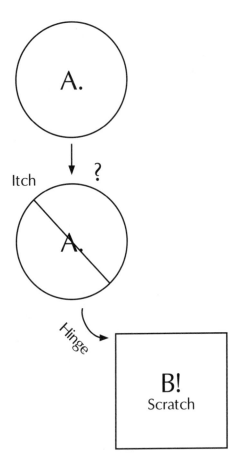

Figure 9.1 • The New Hearing Form

Chapter 9

New Hearing Sermons

The New Hearing form is helpful if the preacher wants to present a view of some issue that goes against a commonly held understanding of the issue. In other words, this sermonic approach is best suited for occasions when the preacher wants to offer a corrective to some view held in the congregation or the cultural environment in which the congregation ministers. The logic used is similar to that of Jesus in the section of the Sermon on the Mount referred to as the "antitheses." This is where Jesus preaches, "You have heard it said . . . , but I say to you . . ." (Matt. 5:21-48). The structure of the logic is:

> *Not A,*
> *thus B.*

The Form

The New Hearing sermon is inductive in mode. The hearers do not know where the preacher is heading at the beginning of the sermon. In fact, the itch is created slowly over the first two major sections of the sermon and the scratch only comes in the third. It is a simple structure to use.

Usually the form does not require a separate introduction because the *opening movement* serves to introduce the issue at hand. In this section, a common understanding of something is presented. For this sermon form to be effective, the common understanding should be one that is well known to the congregation and most likely held by many of those gathered. Thus, it is important that the description of the common understanding be a fair one. A preacher who caricatures a position with which his hearers agree and with which he is going to disagree is not going to get a sympathetic understanding. No one will be persuaded if that in which they believe is mocked. This movement should take about one-fourth of the sermon.

Nevertheless, the preacher must structure the description in the opening section so that it leads up to a *plausible question* concerning this common understanding. This question then leads the preacher into the *middle movement* in which he rejects the usual interpretation. This should take about the same time as the first movement. The idea is to convince the hearers that there is good reason to reconsider their belief or value. Similar to the tone needed for the opening section, the appeal must be sympathetic to the hearers' investment in the common understanding. The rejection, therefore, cannot in any way ridicule the common understanding. It can include either or both logical and emotional appeals, but it must be pastoral in tone, even if the issue under consideration is a prophetic one or one about which the preacher has especially strong feelings. One can be passionate and compassionate at the same time.

This does not mean that humor cannot be used in the middle section. Humor can be disarming. It can help hearers let their defenses down, as long as they do not experience themselves as the target of the humor. In other words, humor that uses indirection can be helpful in supporting (not replacing) a rejection of a misunderstanding, but humor that makes fun of a view and those who hold it will be counterproductive and potentially hurtful.

The rejection of the common understanding leaves a gap that the preacher needs to fill. If the first two sections have worked, the hearers are waiting for, wanting, indeed needing an alternate view to be offered. The *closing movement* of the sermon, therefore, is the climax of the sermon and should be its longest section. It should take about half of the time of the sermon. Here the direction of the sermon shifts from deconstruction to offering a constructive theological or ethical proposal. Part of constructing a consistent Christian worldview requires the preacher to provide imagery that makes the proposal offered here real to the world. Imagery should play a vital role in the first two movements of the sermon, but it is absolutely essential here. The vitality of a proposal that the preacher hopes to be persuasive over against views she wants a congregation to lay aside depends on the word becoming flesh, if you will. She must offer the listeners an experience of the sermonic claim, not just an argument for it.

Having looked at the parts of the New Hearing form, we can now recognize that there are primarily two types of misunderstanding that this sermonic approach addresses. The first is a common misinterpretation of the biblical text for the sermon. Consider a sermon on the story of the widow's offering in the Temple that is found at the end of Jesus' Temple discourse in Mark 12:41-44.

A: The opening section could present the way preachers usually use this text—lifting up the widow as a role model for stewardship in the church.

Not A: In the second section the preacher can back up just one verse (12:40) to show that Jesus mentions that widows are victims of oppression by religious authorities. She can show how Jesus' posture ("over against the treasury"; cf. 13:3 where Jesus sits "over against" the Temple) is one of prophetic critique. This doesn't seem to be an example story at all.

B: Instead of hearing Jesus' word that the woman has put in all she had, her very livelihood, as praise, the preacher shows that it should be heard as condemnation of religious institutions that demand an unjustifiable sacrifice from the poor instead of meeting their needs. Imagery of televangelists living large on the backs of the widows, the unemployed, and the desperate could be used to show that Jesus' critique is anything but outdated. However, a sermon's purpose is to offer good news. Judgment must be turned around so that it becomes calling. So the preacher turns the negative critique around and names the proper role of religious institutions implied in the story: a key element of the church's vocation is to alleviate the suffering of the "widows" of the world. At this point she offers a positive image of a community of faith that lives out the compassion envisioned in this text to conclude the sermon.

The second, and more common, type of misunderstanding a New Hearing sermon can be used to address involves a theological or ethical perspective. In this situation the biblical text is used in a very different fashion than in the previous example. Here, the preacher wants to take on a common theological understanding and uses the biblical text as the hinge to move the congregation to a new position. The text serves as a lens for a "new viewing" of the issue at hand. Imagine a sermon in which the preacher wants to offer a different understanding of Christian eschatology or apocalypticism than he has heard mentioned in some Sunday school classes recently.

A: The opening section could begin by discussing Tim LaHaye and Jerry Jenkins's "Left Behind" series and the way it follows in the path of earlier works like Hal Lindsey's *The Late, Great Planet Earth* by offering a so-called literal, dispensational interpretation of the apocalyptic texts in the New Testament.

Not A: In the middle section, the preacher will try to persuade the congregation to reject the hermeneutic just displayed by teaching them how apocalyptic literature and imagery really functioned in the ancient world. By drawing on the evocative power of dreamlike imagery, apocalyptic literature named an experience of evil in the world and called for trust in God's ultimate sovereignty, instead of predicting a literal, chronological sequence of events.

B: The final section, then, can open by turning to a specific apocalyptic passage in the New Testament and reading it through the lens of this hermeneutic of experience and move toward offering imagery that presents a person or community which lives or lived by trusting the future to God while striving to be faithful in the present.

Evaluation of the Form

In a postmodern climate where many Christians think of the faith in terms of individually held beliefs that need not be developed into a consistent theological worldview, the New Hearing form can be a useful tool for preachers. To help congregations think through the implications of their beliefs to the point of being willing to change them is a significant gift preachers can give to those growing in the faith. By engaging seriously a view that they want to reject, preachers using this form do not engage in an authoritarian approach to the role of the preacher in shaping the theology of the congregation, but instead take seriously the desire and need of people to be addressed intelligently and recognize the authority of the hearers to make theological judgments by offering them serious arguments to consider.

It is often said that we live in a day when there is much biblical, theological, historical, and liturgical illiteracy among Christians. One cause of this may surely be the shift in preaching that occurred over the last half century, moving from argument/persuasive types of discourse to experiential types. The importance of this corrective should not be dismissed. However, with the corrective came a diminishing of the didactic role of the pulpit. Never more than today must preaching and teaching enter into holy matrimony to produce children of the faith. The New Hearing form allows this partnership to flourish.

This strength is also the form's weakness. Its focus on information and argumentation means this is a sermon form directed primarily to the hearers' intellect. The New Hearing form has the potential to open minds but will rarely do much to move the heart. It will more likely offer insight into the gospel than an experience of it. Any chance for the latter depends on how imagery is used in the closing section.

Case Study: 1 Kings 19:1-15a

Given that the New Hearing form offers insight into some aspect of the faith, some corrective to theological misunderstanding, it has much to offer the sermonic claim I chose for a sermon based on the story of Elijah on Mount Horeb. I chose to use the scene as a lens through which to reject an understanding of "coming to church" to escape from the world and instead to offer a vision of worship as a time and place from which God sends us out to confront and transform the world.

The New Hearing form could serve this claim in either of the ways described earlier, by countering either a misinterpretation of the text or of the mission of the church. For the first the sermons would flow in the following manner:

A: People usually focus on the small, still voice in this text, claiming that God comes to us in our times of need in quiet, comforting ways.

Not A: But God does not offer Elijah comfort. God "calls him out," challenging why he has come to this sacred mountain.

B: God sends Elijah back to the world from which he is trying to escape, just as God sends us out from this worship service.

This approach is not all bad. It does offer a new hearing of the text. To use the form in this way, however, is to tag my real concern on at the end of the sermon. The current context of the hearers only shows up in the last section. This can be corrected some by weaving the biblical imagery with liturgical imagery throughout the sermon in ways that the congregation realizes what is happening. I could speak of Elijah's moving south from the wilderness toward Horeb using language of passing through the narthex to enter the nave. And I could imagine the cave on the mountain furnished with pews, table, and cross and organ music echoing around the stalagmites. The moment in which God calls out Elijah to the opening of the cave and says, "Go, return . . ." would be described using language of the pastor's hands raised in benediction or making the sign of the cross over the people as they are pushed out of the front door into the world of work, politics, relationships—that is, vocation.

The second approach is better, however. Addressing directly the common misunderstanding of worship attendance as a form of escapism, I would put the biblical text in a role of supporting the argument instead of being the focal point of the sermon. The sermon could work in this way:

A: I could begin by describing the ways in which the world is a scary and violent place. Church offers us time away from the world—we come to worship to find "sanctuary" from the troubles "out there." Prayers, songs, and Eucharist in this holy place offer us comfort that allows us to forget what's going on in the profane world.

Not A: While it is appropriate to find comfort in worship, the church should not engage in escapism. A church focused inwardly is nothing more than a country club with a chaplain. I could present imagery of inward-turned churches here.

B: I would use the scriptural text for the day as a hinge toward a positive proposal: Elijah went to Mount Horeb to escape the wrath of the corrupt rulers, but God sent him back to face his fears. When we pray, we pray for the world. When we sing, we sing for the world. When we celebrate the Eucharist, we remember Christ died for the world. We come to church for the benediction—to be sent out as God's prophetic emissaries to confront corruption and oppression and alleviate suffering. I would close with an image of a church that strives to do this.

Diagrammed, the sermon would look something like this:

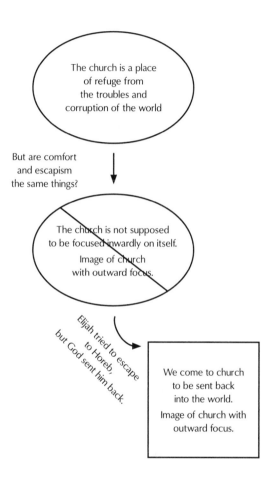

Figure 9.2 • A New Hearing Sermon on 1 Kings 19:1-15a

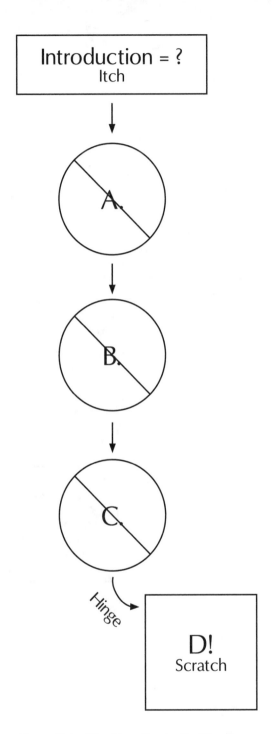

Figure 10.1 • The Negative to Positive Form

Chapter 10

Negative to Positive Sermons

This sermonic form is closely related to the New Hearing form described in the previous chapter, both in terms of logic and structure. In the New Hearing, the sermon begins with a view commonly held, moves to a rejection of that view, and closes with a counterproposal. In Negative to Positive sermons, the sermon opens with a question, proceeds through a range of possible answers that the preacher rejects, and then closes by proposing an answer the preacher hopes the congregation will accept.

The Form
The Negative to Positive sermon works inductively. The congregation does not know what the positive proposal will be until the last movement of the sermon. The preacher offers an *opening question* that creates an initial itch and sustains and deepens that itch as she presents and then rejects one answer after another. In other words, the *introduction* of the sermon is the introduction of the question. How long this introduction takes depends on whether the congregation already has the question on their minds and how much it is at the front of their minds. Is the preacher simply naming a question hearers already have or is he trying to get them to ask a question that has not been on their radar screens? Obviously, the second scenario requires a longer introduction. If preacher and congregation are already on the same page concerning the importance of the question (not necessarily the answer), the preacher can simply name the question, frame it to set up what is to follow, and move on. Is there a heaven and a hell? How should Christians view homosexuality? If, on the other hand, the preacher is posing a question that some hearers will be

considering for the first time (or at least considering at the level the preacher wants for the first time), then the preacher must move more slowly at the beginning. What is the meaning of the doctrine of the Trinity? How should Christians view other religions? The congregation may have to be convinced that such a question is existentially important, that the answer to the question will influence their theology, faith, and/or behavior. Use of imagery will be helpful in this endeavor.

The kind of question we pose at the beginning of this sermonic form can vary greatly. It can be *exegetical*, such as, What is Paul's understanding of the resurrection of the body in 1 Corinthians 15? *Doctrinal*, such as, If we accept the scientific view of the world, what does it mean to say God created the world? *Ethical/moral*, such as, What is the role of the Christian in politics? *Spiritual*, such as, Why do we maintain a Lenten discipline? Whatever the question, for this form to work it needs to have *multiple possible answers*. If there are only two options, only yes or no, or only agreement or disagreement, then the preacher should use the New Hearing form. In the Negative to Positive form, on the other hand, there are a number of competing possibilities through which the preacher wishes to wade. The preacher will work through these possibilities one at a time, rejecting each one before moving on to the next.

As noted in the discussion of the rejection of the common understanding of the subject matter in the New Hearing sermon, we must not caricature the positions we reject. We name them in the first place because we assume there are people who hold them, and some of those may be sitting in our pews. To make fun of a position we do not hold belittles those with whom we disagree. To name a position correctly and to show why we reject it invites hearers who hold the position to reconsider and possibly join us in looking for a better answer. Indeed, in this form the rejection of possible answers need not be a full-blown, all-or-nothing rejection. We need not demonstrate that a possible answer has no worth in order to offer a better proposal. We must simply show that there is something about the answer that is not fully satisfactory, that calls for further consideration.

The preacher must leave adequate time for full consideration of the proposed answer—at least a third of the sermon—if the positive answer is to outweigh the multiple negative ones. This means that each possible answer rejected in the Negative to Positive sermon cannot receive the same level of attention as the single one rejected in a New Hearing sermon. The preacher must name the possible answer in just enough detail to do it justice, show quickly why she is not persuaded by that answer, and move on to the next. This process may not involve detailed imagery, but the preacher should seek ways to make sure these options are experienced as real and not leave them in the abstract. Of course, the complexity of both the initial question posed and of the individual answers considered will require different levels of detail. Issues too complex may not be best served by this form.

Usually in this form, a specific reading of the text for the day will serve as the hinge for shifting from negative answers to a positive one. The text obviously may be used throughout the sermon in different ways, but the strongest role is the scriptural support for the *proposed answer* at the end of the sermon. So a creative, exegetical walk though the text will often lead to a direct statement of the proposed answer. The preacher follows this statement of the sermonic claim with an argument that uses the same basic type of logic or the same standard of evaluation presented when rejecting the other answers. In other words, with this sermonic form, we need to make sure we are offering the congregation an orange to compare with oranges. To reject a set of possible answers on one basis and to accept another on a different one is not fair to the issue nor does it really aid the congregation in making a theological or ethical judgment.

While the evaluation needs to be on the same terms, our primary goal in preaching is to offer a constructive view or experience of some aspect of the gospel, not simply to deconstruct views we consider less desirable. So we should be fair to the positions we reject and use the same standard for accepting the answer we propose, but we should also put our best foot forward in this final, positive movement of the sermon. One of the simplest ways to make sure the proposed answer is the climactic point in the sermon is to use the strongest imagery here. Metaphors, stories, testimony, and the like will move the sermon beyond persuasive argumentation to proclamation that has the potential to touch hearers' lives.

Evaluation of the Form
The Negative to Positive form shares the same basic strengths and weaknesses as the New Hearing form. In terms of weakness, the form can leave hearers in their heads and not move them into their hearts or inspire use of hands unless imagery is used well. Of course, the intellectual appeal of this form is also its strength. This form offers hearers, in an age of biblical and theological illiteracy, a model for how theological thinking works itself out. So, not only does the preacher address a significant issue in the sermon, he presents the congregation with a method for reflecting on theological and ethical issues in general.

Case Study: 1 Kings 19:1-15a
To show how the Negative to Positive form might work in for a specific sermon, let us return one final time to the story of Elijah on Mount Horeb.

Remember that exegesis led me to read the text in terms of vocation, and thus I chose to use the scene as a lens through which to interpret an element of the church's mission. Specifically, I plan to draw an analogy between Elijah's fleeing to Mount Horeb and the way some people escape the world by coming to church. I want to counter that understanding of gathering to worship with an analogy drawn from God's recall of Elijah, or God's sending Elijah back down the mountain. While this two-sided analogy was an easy fit for the New Hearing form, the Negative to Positive requires some reorientation of rhetorical strategy but still has promise.

Knowing where I want this sermon to end (with an affirmation of the church's outreach mission based on God's sending Elijah back down the mountain), I have to decide how to begin. Specifically in terms of a Negative to Positive sermon, I have to determine the best way to frame the *opening question* with multiple possible answers to introduce the sermon. One way is straightforward—I could begin by asking, "What is the purpose of the church? What is the church's mission? Why did God give us the church?" This type of question will allow me to name and reject different views of the church I find too self-serving and then to propose the outward-focused mission as the climax.

A second way is more playful and inviting. I could begin with the question, "Do you know what the most important part of worship is?" This question could be unpacked so that it hints that the issue is really about the relation of worship and the church's mission/identity:

I'll bet you got up this morning with the same question on your mind that's been on mine: What's the most important part of worship? No? Really? Well, I've been thinking about it anyway. Of course, I think it's all important. And I think all of the different parts of worship fit together to make an important whole. But different churches with different senses of their purpose and mission and identity emphasize different parts of worship. Contemporary seeker services emphasize praise music because it invites an individual, devotional experience of God. The Roman Catholic Church emphasizes the Eucharist because it is Christ's atoning sacrifice for God's people. What do you think we ought to emphasize? Now the question isn't just, "What is your *favorite* part of worship?" Because some really love the music and others really love the children's time and all of you absolutely adore the sermons. But beyond just what we like, what's the *most important* part of our worship service?

This question creates a playful *itch*. Hearers do not possess a burning question about weighing different parts of the service theologically. Using humor to create the itch invites hearers into the issue but also hints that it may only be a presenting symptom of something more serious to follow. Nevertheless, this way of framing the question allows me to offer some liturgical education as a subtext of the sermon. As I review *rejected answers*, I could walk through different individual elements of the service—invocation, Scripture reading, sermon, creed, table, hymns—describe their purpose, explain why they are most important, and say why they are not most important.

Or, to simplify I could use the headings in the bulletin that follow the four-fold structure of the ordo—Gathering, Proclamation, Response, and Sending Forth. Because I am using Elijah's experience of being sent back down the mountain by God as the turning point for the sermon and am thus going to claim that the Sending Forth best expresses who we are (or are to be), I want to value the first three movements of the ordo but reject them as most important. I could use other parts of the text to unpack these movements playfully:

Gathering = Elijah fleeing from Jezebel and Ahab to Horeb
Proclamation = God speaking in the sheer silence
Response = Elijah's answer to God's question, "Why are you here?"

All of these parts of the service are important but will be rejected on the basis of ways we view them inwardly, serving our purposes (as Elijah sought to meet his needs).

The *hinge* for the sermon will be the discussion of God's recall of Elijah. The prophet seeks to get away from it all, but God sends him back into the middle of it all. Similarly for us, I would argue, the most important part of the worship service is being sent forth. We gather to be sent away. As the sermon turns to the *positive answer*, I would slow down significantly in order to use the Sending Forth as a lens for looking at the real subject matter of the sermon: the outreach aspect of the church's mission. I would describe what God sent Elijah to do and draw parallels with what God calls us to do in our context. And I would use uplifting and inspiring imagery that presents the church as doing just that. (Then I would make sure that the Sending Forth part of the service, on this day and others, grew in importance.)

If we use the flow chart of the Negative to Positive form from the beginning of the chapter and insert our material, it looks like this (see figure 10.2, p. 78):

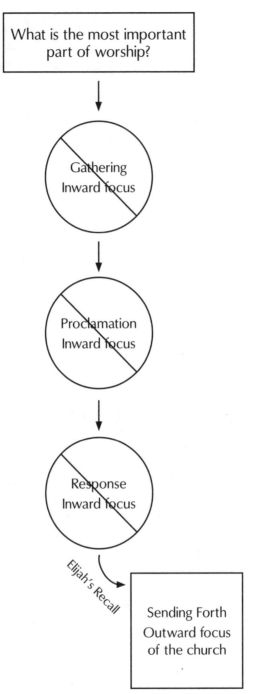

Figure 10.2 • A Negative to Positive Sermon on 1 Kings 19:1-15a

This volume began with a wide-angle glance at some broad issues related to sermonic form and then zoomed in to focus on some specific forms available to preachers each time they step into the pulpit. As I draw this discussion to a close, it is perhaps wise to zoom out again and offer a few pieces of practical advice about learning and using these forms in general. For the sake of homiletical appropriateness, let's make it three points!

First, whether you are a beginning preacher being introduced to these forms for the first time or a more seasoned preacher using the book to learn some new forms, I would suggest trying to master only two or three new forms at a time. Moreover, I suggest using these new forms in a legalistic fashion at first. Learn them well and use them precisely as presented before moving on to the next two pieces of advice. Doing this will place the learned forms securely in your homiletical knapsack so that they are readily available across the span of your preaching ministry.

Second, once you have mastered a form in the way I have laid it out, you should experiment with it, adapting the structure to fit the purposes and convey the content and imagery differently for different sermons. In other words, while you will do well to learn these forms in a legalistic manner initially, you should not consider them to be rhetorical laws for preaching in the long term. What is rhetorically essential for good preaching is unity, movement, and climax. The forms presented in this volume are simply some fundamental ways to focus a sermon and structure the communication in a sensible and stimulating fashion so that it leads the congregation to a climactic impact at the end. On any given occasion, the preacher's intended purpose may best be achieved by changing a classic form into something altogether new. Like an architect, preachers can use these forms as standard foundations upon which to design and build a wide variety of creative structures.

And, third, readers should remember that what is offered here is only a brief foray into the discussion concerning sermonic form. The homiletical discussion of the last four decades has repeatedly raised questions about structure and flow of sermons. Forms chosen for this book are specifically oriented toward an elementary introduction to sermonic structure. There are other forms available and a wide variety of other rhetorical issues that relate to form to be considered (for example, a lot of attention has been given to sermonic form being influenced by the form of the biblical text). As I argued earlier, two sides of the same homiletical coin are consistency of voice Sunday after Sunday and variety of form from week to week. Once the forms in this book are mastered, preachers will do well to engage the wider conversation concerning this element of the *how* of preaching to achieve breadth of form. For this purpose a select bibliography is included below.

In conclusion, form and function are intimately related in all art forms. Thus, the better one shapes the structure of the sermon for the listeners the more effective that sermon will be in offering the congregation the gospel of Jesus Christ in power, beauty, and grace.

For Further Reading

Allen, O. Wesley. *Good News from Tinyville: Stories of Hope and Heart.* St. Louis: Chalice, 1999. Allen offers a collection of story-sermons, along with a discussion of the use of story as the form of the sermon.

Allen, Ronald J., and Gilbert L. Bartholomew. *Preaching Verse by Verse.* Louisville: Westminster John Knox, 2000. Allen and Bartholomew breathe new life into this form of preaching.

Allen, Ronald J., ed. *Patterns of Preaching: A Sermon Sampler.* St. Louis: Chalice, 1998. Allen gathers preachers from across gender, race, and theological lines to demonstrate a wide variety of types of preaching.

Arthurs, Jeffery, and Haddon Robinson. *Preaching with Variety: How to Re-create the Dynamics of Biblical Genres.* Grand Rapids: Kregel, 2007. Similar to Graves and Long (included in this list), Arthurs and Robinson argue that preachers should vary the forms they use in the pulpit in relation to the function of the genre of the text on which they are preaching.

Buttrick, David. *Homiletic: Moves and Structures.* Philadelphia: Fortress Press, 1987. Buttrick discusses a wide variety of homiletical issues in the large book, but his introduction of "moves"—structured episodes within the sermon—has been especially influential on homiletics.

Craddock, Fred B. *As One Without Authority.* Rev. ed. St. Louis: Chalice, 2001. This book, originally published in 1971, radically changed the preaching landscape by inviting preachers to develop sermons that move inductively instead of deductively.

Eslinger, Richard L. *A New Hearing: Living Options in Homiletic Method.* Nashville: Abingdon, 1987. Eslinger draws together and compares those who are considered to be the pillars of the New Homiletic: Charles L. Rice, Fred B. Craddock, Henry H. Mitchell, Eugene L. Lowry, and David Buttrick.

Graves, Mike. *The Sermon as Symphony: Preaching the Literary Forms of the New Testament.* Valley Forge: Judson, 1997. Similar to Arthurs/Robinson and Long (included in this list), Graves argues that preachers should develop form-sensitive sermons, sermons in which the shape of the biblical text has influenced the shape of the sermon.

Hogan, Lucy Lind, and Robert Reid. *Connecting with the Congregation: Rhetoric and the Art of Preaching*. Nashville: Abingdon, 1999. Hogan and Reid attempt to reclaim the importance of rhetorical study for effective congregational preaching.

Long, Thomas G. *Preaching and the Literary Forms of the Bible*. Philadelphia: Fortress Press, 1989. Similar to Graves and Arthurs/Robinson (included in this list), Long discusses how the structure of the sermon can be influenced by the shape of the biblical text.

Lowry, Eugene L. *The Homiletical Plot: The Sermon as Narrative Art Form*. Exp. ed. Louisville: Westminster John Knox, 2001. Lowry proposes a specific narrative structure for inductive sermons.

McClain, William B. *The Liturgy of Zion*. Nashville, Abingdon, 1990. McClain deals with a wide variety of issues related to worship in the African American church, but in chapter 5—"Black Preaching and Its Message: 'Is There Any Word from the Lord?'"—he discusses basic characteristics of black preaching, including elements of form.

Mitchell, Henry H. *Celebration and Experience in Preaching*. Nashville: Abingdon, 1990. While Mitchell introduces the role of celebration in black preaching in earlier works, this book is the most thorough discussion of the climactic element of celebration and how to structure sermons to effect such an experience.

Thomas, Frank A. *They Like to Never Quit Praisin' God: The Role of Celebration in Preaching*. Cleveland: United Church Press, 1997. Thomas expands on Henry H. Mitchell's introduction of celebration as the climax of the sermon, providing specific advice for developing the experience in the congregation.

Wilson, Paul Scott. *The Four Pages of the Sermon: A Guide to Biblical Preaching*. Nashville: Abingdon, 1999. Wilson proposes a sermonic structure that moves from problem to gospel, paralleling the situation in the ancient text and that of the contemporary congregation.

Notes

Chapter 1 • Why Form Matters

1. O. A. Dieter, "Arbor Picta: The Medieval Tree of Preaching," *Quarterly Journal of Speech* 51 (1965): 123–44.

2. R. E. C. Browne, *The Ministry of the Word* (London: SCM, 1958).

3. H. Grady Davis, *Design for Preaching* (Philadelphia: Muhlenberg, 1958), 9.

4. Ibid., 15.

5. The pillars of the New Homiletic are Charles L. Rice, Fred B. Craddock, Henry H. Mitchell, Eugene L. Lowry, and David Buttrick. They are reviewed in Richard L. Eslinger, *A New Hearing: Living Options in Homiletical Method* (Nashville: Abingdon, 1987).

6. See Mary Lin Hudson and Mary Donovan Turner, *Saved from Silence: Finding Women's Voice in Preaching* (St. Louis: Chalice, 1999) and David J. Schlafer, *Your Way with God's Word: Discovering Your Distinctive Preaching Voice* (Cambridge: Cowley, 1995).

7. See Marvin A. McMickle, *Shaping the Claim: Moving from Text to Sermon,* Elements of Preaching (Minneapolis: Fortress Press, 2008).

Chapter 2 • Unity, Movement, and Climax

1. On the shift from narratives to movies as paradigmatic for preaching, see Paul Scott Wilson, *The Four Pages of the Sermon: A Guide to Biblical Preaching* (Nashville: Abingdon, 1999), 9–12.

2. For Lowry's discussion of the movement from itch to scratch, see *The Homiletical Plot: The Sermon as Narrative Art Form,* exp. ed. (Louisville: Westminster John Knox, 2001 [originally pub. Nashville: Abingdon, 1971]), 15–21.

3. Lucy Atkinson Rose, *Sharing the Word: Preaching in the Roundtable Church* (Louisville: Westminster John Knox, 1997), 84–85, critiques the idea found in transformative preaching (the New Homiletic) that the same hearers can be transformed week after week.

4. The climax of each sermon need not always be dramatic turning points for hearers because sermons work cumulatively in the transformation of hearers; see O. Wesley Allen, Jr., *The Homiletic of All Believers: A Conversational Approach* (Louisville: Westminster John Knox, 2005), 51–57.

Chapter 3 • Case Study: 1 Kings 19:1-15a

1. This summary of exegetical observations does not show the process by which those observations were made. On exegesis for preaching, see Mary F.

Foskett, *Interpreting the Bible: Exegetical Approaches for Preaching*, Elements of Preaching (Minneapolis: Fortress Press, forthcoming).

Chapter 4 • Propositional Lesson Sermons

1. Cleophus J. LaRue, "Two Ships Passing in the Night," in *What's the Matter with Preaching Today?* ed. Mike Graves (Louisville: Westminster John Knox, 2004), 130–32.

Chapter 5 • Exegesis—Interpretation—Application Sermons

1. See O. Wesley Allen Jr., *Reading the Synoptic Gospels: Basic Methods for Interpreting Matthew, Mark, and Luke* (St. Louis: Chalice, 2000).

2. On the use of hermeneutical analogy in preaching, see Stephen Farris, *Preaching That Matters: The Bible and Our Lives* (Louisville: Westminster John Knox, 1998).

3. See Ronald J. Allen, *Thinking Theologically: The Preacher as Theologian*, Elements of Preaching (Minneapolis, Fortress Press, 2008).

Chapter 6 • Verse-by-Verse Sermons

1. The most thorough defense and explanation of this type of preaching in recent years is found in Ronald J. Allen and Gilbert L. Bartholomew, *Preaching Verse by Verse* (Louisville: Westminster John Knox, 2000).

2. On the interaction of imagery throughout a sermon, see David Buttrick's discussion of the "image grid" in *Homiletic: Moves and Structures* (Philadelphia: Fortress Press, 1987).

Chapter 7 • The Four Pages Sermon

1. Paul Scott Wilson, *The Four Pages of the Sermon: A Guide to Biblical Preaching* (Nashville: Abingdon, 1999).

2. See David L. Bartlett, "Showing Mercy," in *What's the Matter with Preaching Today,* ed. Mike Graves (Louisville: Westminster John Knox, 2004), 23–35.

Chapter 8 • Valley Sermons

1. Eugene L. Lowry, *The Homiletical Plot: The Sermon as Narrative Art Form,* exp. ed. (Louisville: Westminster John Knox, 2000 [originally pub. Nashville: Abingdon, 1971]); in his afterword in the expanded edition, Lowry revises the diagram plot slightly to see the Aha! and Whee! movements as nearly a single movement.

2. William B. McClain, *Come Sunday: The Liturgy of Zion* (Nashville: Abingdon, 1990), 62–70.

3. As noted in the previous chapter, see David L. Bartlett, "Showing Mercy," in *What's the Matter with Preaching Today,* ed. Mike Graves (Louisville: Westminster John Knox, 2004), 23–35.